THE HOME BUSINESS REVOLUTION'S
GREATEST
ENTREPRENEURS

VOLUME TWO

*The exclusive interviews from
Six-Figure Income Magazine*

The Home Business Revolution's Greatest Entrepreneurs

Printed in the United States of America

ISBN 0-9669615-1-X

Published by
Carson Services, Inc.
P.O. Box 4785, Lincoln, NE 68504
(402) 434-8480

DEDICATION

To my mother, Eao. *Life has dealt you some tough blows, taking away those closest in your life, far before their time. Yet you did not wither. You refused to give in to bitterness. You did not lose your faith. You may not have known it, but your strength and courage have always been a great and enduring inspiration to me. For this, and many other inspirations, blessings, and gifts that only a mother can give, I thank you, Mom. I love you.*

GC

CONTENTS

# INTRODUCTION

I still remember it clearly. It was 1985, I was 23, and I had just discovered two books that would go on to have a huge impact on my life and the business I was about to start.

The first book was *The Magic of Thinking Big* by David J. Schwartz. That book opened my eyes, and the other, the all-time success classic, *Think and Grow Rich* by Napoleon Hill, sent me *soaring* with the knowledge that I had within me spectacular, untapped talents and unlimited potential.

I was also very inspired by Mr. Hill's mission – to interview the richest, most successful people in the world, and to document what it was they had in common, so that this knowledge could be shared with anyone who had the drive and desire to achieve greatness.

In 1998, when I began formulating ideas for a new magazine that I wanted to publish, my "old friend" *Think and Grow Rich* emerged in my thinking. I knew instantly what I wanted to do. Like Napoleon Hill, I would shine a light on ultra-successful entrepreneurs, so that others could learn from them and apply that knowledge to their lives and businesses.

In your hands you hold detailed profiles of 24 incredible and very successful individuals. Indeed! Laid out for you to emulate are the very strategies, philosophies, and actual techniques they used to achieve their mammoth success – a literal wealth of ideas, insights, and guidance by the best of the best. *Enjoy!*

Gery Carson

Glen Brink

Age: 54

Family: Single

Education: Three years of college

Employees: None

Year Started Business: Went full time in network marketing in 1979

Type of Business: Mail Order/Network Marketing

Got In Business For Himself Because: Glen has a Masters Degree in Statistics and found himself in the world of computers and a technical work environment. "One day on the job in front of my computer terminal, I noticed that my interests and my very life was gradually moving away from everyday reality and further and further into the electronic machines and computer languages of my professional career. I was a natural geek, but when I recognized the limitations involved, I decided then and there to find activities to bring me closer to people. Now I like creativity, change, and personal growth."

Best Month (gross revenue): $52,000

Hours Worked Per Week During Start-Up: Every waking hour

Hours Worked Per Week Now: Still works 90% of his time establishing his business and celebrating with his distributors. "It is a lifestyle we're building, not just a job."

Favorite Business Magazines: Scans all the magazines and newsletters he gets—no favorites.

Favorite Business Books/Authors: Listens to books on tape and taped lectures.

Best Thing About Being Self Employed: Freedom and choice. "I became so independent that I was no longer good employee material."

Relaxes By: Watching movies; also studies and teaches personal development and self-change technology

Favorite Part of His Business: Helping people expand their horizons

Least Favorite Part of His Business: Appointments and deadlines

Stays Fit By: Using a Rebounder and attending Network Chiropractic

Heroes: "Harry Palmer is my hero for pointing me in the direction of growth and change. All of the leaders I work with are heroes in their ability to help establish a better world. Jerry Clark is a primary example of the American rags-to-riches story we all love so well."

Admired Companies: Modern flexible organizations like Star's Edge R&D, Royal BodyCare, and Wired magazine

Contact Glen at: (303) 442-6460

Ray Gebauer

Age: 47

Family: Diana (wife), 41; Children: Ray J. Gebauer, 24; Scott Gebauer, 22; John, 19; Jacob, 9

Education: Five years of college

Employees: None

Year Started Business: 1994

Type of Business: Network Marketing

Got In Business For Himself Because: Liked being his own boss and did not want to settle for working for someone else

Best Month (gross revenue): $100,000

Hours Worked Per Week During Start-Up: 80

Hours Worked Per Week Now: 60+

Favorite Business Magazines: Upline Journal

Favorite Business Books/Authors: Mach II with your Hair on Fire—Richard Brooke; Becoming a Person of Influence—John C. Maxwell; Living with Passion—Tony Robbins

Best Thing About Being Self Employed: Personal freedom

Relaxes By: Hiking

Favorite Part of His Business: Writing and training

Least Favorite Part of His Business: Paperwork

Stays Fit By: Using the Rebounder (mini trampoline) and taking walks

Heroes: Jesus, Mike Bickle (a pastor in Kansas City), and John Wimber (founder of the Vineyard churches)

Admired Companies: Mannatech, OxyFresh, New Image International

Favorite Quotes: When the why is strong enough, the how will take care of itself; For things to change, you've got to change—Jim Rohn; Guard your heart, for out of it flows the springs of life—Solomon

Books & Tapes By Ray Gebauer: The Freedom Workshop, Leadership Development Workship, and How I Went From Being a Business Failure to Making a Million Dollars as a Mannatech Maniac

Contact Ray at: (888) 882-8949

Joseph P. Lemire

Age: 58

Family: Ruthann (wife); Children: Deborah, 36; Kimberlee, 35; Joseph, 32; Paul 28; Michael, 25; Grandchildren: Adam, 5; Kyle, 4; Rachel, 2; Austin, 9 mos.

Education: High school

Employees: None

Year Started Business: 1994

Type of Business: Network marketing

Best Month (gross revenue): What many people earn in a year

Hours Worked Per Week During Start-Up: 20 hours

Hours Worked Per Week Now: "My work is my lifestyle…travel, work, play, recruit, and sell!"

Favorite Business Magazines: Entrepreneur; Success

Favorite Business Books/Authors: Think & Grow Rich—Napoleon Hill; Be My Guest—Conrad Hilton; The Power of Positive Thinking—Normal Vincent Peale

Relaxes By: Playing gold, hunting pheasant and deer, and spending time with family

Favorite Part of His Business: On the recruiting end, the satisfaction of opening doors for people to earn extra income and stretch and grow from the experience of doing something beyond what they through was possible. On the sales side, the satisfaction of providing a service that will someday be the norm—like health insurance.

Least Favorite Part of His Business: The disappointment of seeing someone who really needs the Pre-Paid Legal service turn it down.

Stays Fit By: Walking vigorously every day

Heroes: His mother and father for their integrity and believing in him; his wife Ruthann for sticking with him through thick and thin; and his children for treating him like a hero

Admired Companies: Hilton Hotel Chain, McDonald's, Chrysler Corporation

Favorite Quotes: I have never met a lucky, lazy person—Allen E. Paulson; If you don't plow, you don't get paid—William E. Bailey

Contact Joseph at: (727) 586-0424

Jean Lewis

Age: Over 21

Family: Ron (husband)—"The wind beneath my wings"

Education: One year business college; cosmetology license

Employees: One

Year Started Business: 1978

Type of Business: Network Marketing; Image Direction

Best Month (gross revenue): $28,000

Hours Worked Per Week During Start-Up: 40 to 50 hours

Hours Worked Per Week Now: 25 to 35 hours

Favorite Business Magazines: Wealth Building Magazine; Home Business Magazine; Kiplinger's Personal Finance Magazine

Favorite Business Books/Authors: "The Bible is the best business book," (Book of Proverbs); The Greatest Salesman in the World—Og Mandino; Think & Grow Rich—Napoleon Hill

Best Thing About Being Self Employed: "I wake up when I want to and go where I want to go. And I don't have to worry about if it will cost too much to do it."

Relaxes By: Shopping, swimming, taking long walks, reading

Favorite Part of Her Business: Being her own boss and telling Jean what to do and when to do it. Being in the position to help others achieve their dreams

Least Favorite Part of Her Business: Talking to people who have a great need for extra cash but can't make the decision that may change their lives financially, even when they have just been offered a no-risk opportunity

Heroes: God

Admired Companies: Microsoft; Cutting Edge Media; Carson Services, Inc.

Favorite Quotes: Ask not what your country can do for you, but what you can do for your country—John F. Kennedy; You will never get a second chance to make a first impression.

Contact Jean at: (941) 698-0444

Anne Rooney

Age: 70

Family: Pat (husband); Children: Debbie, Greg, and Gail; Nine grandchildren

Education: One year of college

Employees: None

Year Started Business: 1993

Type of Business: Network Marketing

Best Month (gross revenue): $35,000

Hours Worked Per Week During Start-Up: 10 to 20 hours

Hours Worked Per Week Now: 20 hours

Favorite Business Magazines: Upline Journal, Success, Network Marketing Magazine

Favorite Business Books/Authors: The Bible; Being The Best You Can Be— John Kalench

Best Thing About Being Self Employed: The quality of life it provides and being able to help put some of their grandchildren through college

Relaxes By: Going away for the weekend or for a week, reading, and just taking it easy

Favorite Part of Her Business: "Being around people we like, and helping them reach their goals."

Least Favorite Part of Her Business: "Being around people who can't see a vision."

Stays Fit By: Walking, working out at the spa

Favorite Quotes: Tomorrow is always a better day—Dale Carnegie; Believe in yourself and have faith in your abilities and with self confidence you can succeed—Norman Vincent Peale

Contact Anne at: (253) 845-1873

Eileen Silva

Age: 51

Family: Taylor (husband); Children: Katie Jo, 28; Trey, 19

Education: Master's Degree

Employees: 4

Year Started Business: 1984

Type of Business: Writing, training, and network marketing

Best Month (gross revenue): $83,000

Hours Worked Per Week During Start-Up: 100+ hours

Hours Worked Per Week Now: Varies

Favorite Business Magazines: Money Makers Monthly, Network Marketing Lifestyles, Upline Journal

Favorite Business Books/Authors: The Corporate Mystic—Gay Hendricks; Seven Spiritual Laws of Success— Deepak Chopra; Think and Grow Rich— Napoleon Hill

Relaxes By: Going to spas and on cruises, walking, reading

Favorite Part of Her Business: Talking on the phone, doing health consultations, doing radio and television interviews and training

Least Favorite Part of Her Business: Dealing with negative thinkers

Stays Fit By: Walking, working out

Admired Companies: Nordstrom's (for service emphasis), Microsoft (for creative genius of management, profit margins as well as product promotion), and First Fitness International (for product effectiveness and motor dedicated to "outlove and outserve the competition.")

Favorite Quotes: Your dreams are what you would do, own or become if your life had no limits—Charles Givens; The greatest discovery of my generation is that a human being can alter his life by altering his attitude of mind—William James; What would you attempt to do if you knew you could not fail?—Robert Schulle

Contact Eileen at: (817) 424-5204

The Interviews

Glen Brink
(GB)

Ray Gebauer
(RG)

Joseph P. Lemire
(JPL)

Jean Lewis
(JL)

Anne Rooney
(AR)

Eileen Silva
(ES)

GETTING STARTED:

I'm starting a home business next month. I have a maximum of $3,000 in start-up capital. Where should I invest it?

GB: First learn how to use a proven system. Then invest your dollars in the best way to maximize that system for you personally. To get the most leverage from your expenses, use your dollars to make up for your current limitations.

RG: $2,000 in product, $500 in training and recruiting supplies, and $500 to travel to a major event by the company.

JPL: Spend as little as possible on your start-up requirements; use most of it as back up.

JL: Study some of the success stories in your opportunity magazines. See what they started with and, if possible, find out how they became successful with a small amount of startup capital. Until you do your homework, leave your money in the bank.

AR: You need approximately $2,500 to invest in products to use yourself and to show to people, as we don't stock the products. You will need approximately another $200 for tools such as tapes, books, videos, etc.

ES: In YOURSELF!!! (trade magazines, books and tapes, personal development work), in technology necessities (like 3-way calling), in supplies (business cards, product, samples, brochures), in promotional things like ads or in training by someone who is successful in your business already; and in lunch tabs for people you can mastermind with. The best way to quickly catapult to success is to not reinvent the wheel.

I've just started a home business. My spouse has given me six months to make it work. Any advice?

GB: Stop taking advice from people without experience. Ask someone who has been successful. If they tell you to forget it, maybe there's something to their opinion. Patience is a sure sign of a successful business person, not quick try/fail get-rich-quick approaches. I recommend a spouse that knows a college degree takes years, and successful careers only begin after an education has been completed.

RG: Get an agreement on what "make it work" means. Creating a full-time income is not realistic for most people to achieve within 6 months. But $500 to $1,000 a month is feasible. The best way would be to make a four-year commitment to the business with an attitude of "doing whatever it takes, as long as it takes."

JPL: Focus on earning money on a daily basis. Evaluate your progress weekly.

JL: I think the spouse should be told that "Rome wasn't built in a day." And a long term, profitable business cannot be built in six months. With the clear understanding that it will more than likely take longer than six months, go forward and do the best you can. At least try to be in the black in six months.

AR: Work it consistently.

ES: Do not polarize your spouse by antagonizing him or her. If you will enroll your spouse into creating a little dreams list for you of what would make him or her happy and then do your best to deliver on the list with your income from the business, you will go a long ways towards melting resistance. Be sure you are mentoring with people who are already where you see yourself. Visualize your success. Be clear on a realistic evaluation of what success after six months would look like (P.S. It wouldn't look like my current income!).

They say it takes money to make money. Should I try to get a small-business loan for my start-up capital or just try to get by with my own limited finances?
GB: I'd bet you already have all the financing you need. Although one of my friends did get a part-time job riding outside on a trash truck during the winter in Wisconsin to accumulate funds for a distributor kit. He truly proved that he didn't need a loan. And he proved successful. People given a kit usually fail.
RG: In general, it is good to borrow money if you need the help. You will be more serious and committed. I borrowed $1,900 from my mother's credit card as a cash advance to buy product. I'm glad I did, and I paid her back within 30 days as I had promised.
JPL: Depending on the type of business. If it is one that needs inventory, you cannot be undercapitalized.
JL: That really depends on how limited your startup capital is. Sometimes, a small business loan will give you a lot more leverage and peace of mind to concentrate on growing and developing the business. If you need it, go for it! If not, no!
AR: Try to just get by with your limited finances.
ES: I am a big believer in good, sound money management. Since I was vice president of two of Charles Givens' companies (THE financial guru of the 80's), I advocate using what you have in the way of resources (not just money but also time, energy, connections, etc.). You can work smarter, not harder, by leveraging other peoples' time and money with a little creative thinking. For example, a UPS truck driver in my business was able to collect enough drop-ship retail sales to promote himself to the top discount level. Net cost: about $20 in brochures and quite a few hours of promotion at truck stops. Fortunately, with the business I'm in, you can get started for practically nothing, and everyone has an equal shot at the brass ring.

Do you consider yourself an early adopter of new technology?
GB: No, just a frequent dabbler.
RG: Yes.
JPL: No.
JL: Yes.
AR: Yes.
ES: No.

If you use a toll-free phone number, what is the primary use for it?
GB: I use a toll-free line in recruiting professionals who expect me to have one. It also makes my advertising dollar go further by increasing the response percentages.
RG: For outgoing recorded messages.
JPL: Recruiting and selling merchandise.

JL: Ad response and product sales.
AR: For my distributors to contact me and any new prospects that I may get.
ES: Orders resulting from radio and television talk shows.

Describe your computer and peripherals used...
GB: Windows 95, ArcList, Microsoft Office software; a scanner, letter-quality printer, and WinFax Pro.
JL: A Pentium II Computer, Windows 98, 40X CD ROM, Microsoft Works, Epson Stylus Printer, and scanner.
ES: I'm on shaky ground here. My job is to pay for all the toys, and it's the staff's job to use them. But I know we have several IBM compatibles with Windows 98, a scanner, and colored printers. Our latest toy is a Lanier state-of-the-art printer and copier wired to the computer.

What software do you consider in the "must-have" category?
GB: No software is essential except between your ears.
JL: Microsoft Works.
ES: Microsoft Office, AOL, and QuickBooks

What other technologies, if any, do you use in your business?
GB: Travel and reading are my "toys."
RG: Cellular phone, hand held PC, lap top computer.
JPL: Cellular phone.
JL: Cellular phone, mini tape recorder.
AR: Cellular phone.
ES: I have my own phone system, an on-hold entertainment feature, total estate and business complex intercom feature, a cell phone, Palm Pilot, a phone in the steering wheel of my Lexus (now I do like that!), a nationwide 800 number.

If you use the World Wide Web, name up to five personal favorite business URLs our readers can benefit from:
GB: www.members.aol.com/glenbrink
RG: www.mlm911.com; www.fortunenow.com; www.upline.com.
JL: www.mmmonthly.com.
ES: Amazon.com is my favorite.

Of all the technology you use, rank the top three:
GB: Telephone, word processing/typewriter, fax.
RG: Phone, computer, training tapes.
JPL: Voice mail, fax-on-demand, cellular phone.
JL: Phone, fax, computer.
AR: Telephone, fax, computer.
ES: Telephone, computer with e-mail and fax.

Do you market on the Internet?
GB: No.
RG: No.
JPL: No.
JL: Not Yet.
AR: No. We don't use the Web to advertise for leads, but we give out a catalog to our customers with our name and ID number that they can use to order on the CAP system in the Nikken Website, www.nikken.com
ES: We send people to our Website and get credibility checks from editors there.

Approximately what % of your sales originate from this marketing?
ES: Less than 10%, but it is more of an enhancing thing. Certainly e-mail has become a major form of rapid updating and communication and marketing for interviews.

Do you use direct mail?
GB: Yes. I specialize in direct mail (DM) because of my background and because many of my business leaders want to use direct mail—and we do it successfully. DM requires technical skills while MLM has historically required personal skills. It's rare to successfully blend those two skills. Most who have tried this marriage have failed; they usually end up blaming the tool instead of learning to use the tool appropriately. They blame "the tape system" or the list brokers or even mail order itself instead of recognizing their own failure to learn the required skills and build a system that works, like we do. Direct mail is a career path, not just a simple "business in a box." Classified ads for inquiries are much simpler and that's why so many MLMers use them
RG: No.
JPL: Some; I send newsletters to key people and follow-up on prospects.
JL: Yes, through postcards and sales opportunity letters.
AR: Very Little. We use phone leads from qualified MLM lead generations, plus we also buy space for booths at fairs, big events, etc.
ES: Yes, through ads and phone follow-ups and, occasionally, promotional mailings.

Approximately what % of your sales originate from this marketing?
GB: 98%.
JPL: Small percentage.
JL: 20-30%.
ES: Less than 10% originate this way, but we use direct marketing as a support vehicle in over 50% of our retail sales.

Do you use print media (e.g. magazines, newspapers, card decks)?
GB: Yes, through occasional Ads.
RG: No.
JPL: Yes. We recruit using ads in magazines.
JL: Yes, with small magazine and newspaper ads.
AR: Yes. The only print media we use is ads in the yellow pages of the telephone directory, which has been quite profitable. We also put up posters and business cards in certain areas like business spas, health places, etc.
ES: Yes, in editorials, ads, and articles (I write for numerous publications and am interviewed frequently in all types of health and fitness magazines).

Approximately what % of your sales originate from this marketing?

GB: 1%.

JL: 10-12%.

ES: Largest majority of all sales originate from media (which includes radio and television)—more than 50%.

Do you use radio and/or TV advertising?

GB: No.

RG: No.

JPL: No.

JL: No, because of the expense involved. However, as a nationally known makeup artist, I have appeared on many local, as well as national, TV shows. In addition, I have done a few radio shows and they have created a lot of attention for whichever business I was promoting.

AR: No.

ES: Not advertising, but I do media appearances frequently. I do very well through shows -- one of my favorite ways to build the business. It's a little hard to be accurate, but I estimate that 30-40% of our sales could generate from the shows.

What other kinds of marketing do you utilize?

GB: I try all new methods.

RG: Buying leads.

JPL: Referral Marketing.

JL: I use press releases and do a lot of Image Direction Seminars that teach skincare and makeup, etc.

AR: Buy prospects lists, get referrals, and sell to the cold market.

ES: I use my software technology to sell thousands of dollars in products every month, I market it to health professionals. We do trade shows occasionally; I make presentations to groups and professionals. I use my book as a rather high-ticket business card, and I have a distinctive photo business card that attracts business for me.

Do you recommend using a toll-free number in advertising? Why or why not?

GB: Yes, for the increased response.

RG: Yes.

JPL: Yes, for a better response.

JL: Yes, but only on the first contact.

ES: Sometimes. I don't use it myself because I think it attracts the tire-kickers. It is very expensive and gives an inexperienced person a false sense of ad response. Lots of lonely people call just to amuse themselves or to compare their company to the competition.

Where do you market?

GB: I market nationally with prospecting and training internationally.

RG: Locally, nationally, and internationally.

JPL: Locally and nationally.

JL: Locally, nationally, and internationally.

AR: Mostly in our local area. But recently, we've gone national, as our products and company are becoming better known.

ES: Locally, nationally, and internationally—with the bulk of our marketing done nationally.

Technology Utilized

	Fax*	Fax-on-Demand	Toll-Free	Voice Mail	Computer	Email	Internet	Website	Email Auto-Responders
Glen Brink	✓	✓	✓	✓	✓	✓	✓	✓	
Ray Gebauer	✓	✓	✓	✓	✓	✓	✓		
Joseph P. Lemire	✓	✓	✓				✓	✓	
Jean Lewis	✓	✓	✓	✓	✓	✓	✓		
Anne Rooney	✓	✓	✓	✓	✓	✓	✓	✓	
Eileen Silva	✓	✓	✓	✓	✓	✓	✓	✓	✓

* Dedicated fax line

THE HOME OFFICE:

How should someone set up their home office to maximize its effectiveness?
GB: Simple and task oriented.
RG: Have a private space.
JPL: Keep your office setup simple and not too comfortable!
JL: If possible, keep your home office away from other household distractions. Make sure you are fully equipped to do your business efficiently and professionally. If possible, have a separate business line installed in the office so calls do not have to be made or received in the den, kitchen or bedroom, where it is not conducive to doing business. Have call waiting or voice message so your line is never busy when someone calls you. Invest in a fax machine. The office is where you will be spending a great deal of time. If it isn't organized and set up with professionalism, you will set yourself up for failure.
AR: We have our office set up in our home, which is paid for by Nikken, Inc. on a special home bonus. We have a computer, fax, three telephone numbers, copy machine, and filing cabinets. We also have a huge family room where we do business training and wellness meetings, etc.
ES: Separate from living quarters; fully loaded with necessary equipment and supplies for peak efficiency.

Are there any ground rules you've established for yourself, family, etc. for operating at home successfully?
GB: Be able to turn it off and enjoy life.
RG: Don't let things distract you but be flexible.
JPL: The hours you spend in your office...work time! The household is set up so that you appear to have left. Keeping this space of time sacred keeps you focused.
JL: Yes, I keep a "to do" list daily and try to accomplish as much of it as possible. I discourage friend or neighbor visits during my work time. I really try to run my business like a business should be run.
AR: Between 8:30 and 11:30 am, I'm not to be disturbed so I can work on the phone.
ES: Yes. Do NOT answer the phone at inappropriate times. We also keep our estate neat in main areas and not work scattered. Additionally I try to be dressed by noon (ha ha).

Do you consider working at home an advantage or disadvantage to your business overall?
GB: Big advantage.
RG: A huge advantage.
JPL: Definite Advantage.
JL: A great advantage. I'm known everywhere as a makeup artist. I don't dare go out without my best face on. But at home, there's no need for makeup and no dress code!
AR: Advantage.
ES: Incredible advantage.

MANAGEMENT STYLE:

Do you farm out any of your work?
GB: Yes. I farm out any work as needed to grow my organization. But a hands-on approach is the soundest way until you grow into a situation demanding outsourcing.
RG: Yes.
JPL: No.
JL: No, I do not. When I have a giant project to do, I use help but only on a temporary basis. I'm very fortunate because my husband is a CPA and he handles all the administrative work. Plus, he's great on the computer. He makes my business cards, brochures, flyers, etc.
AR: We designate a lot of our distributors to set up their own meetings, etc.
ES: Yes.

What parts should never be farmed out?
GB: No work is too sacred to be farmed out. But it takes experience to know when it can work.
RG: Administration and paperwork.
ES: Public Relations is always farmed out, and occasionally, ad designs, mail campaigns, all financial services, tape duplication, huge printing jobs, and tool designs. We would never farm out personal communication with our distributors.

Do you encourage or discourage...partnerships?
GB: I discourage legal partnerships, but encourage creative forms of teamwork.
RG: Encourage.
JPL: Discourage.
JL: The only partnership I encourage is between husband and wife.
AR: For a spouse only.
ES: Discourage!

Do you encourage or discourage...hiring family members?
GB: Hiring family members is often used as a simple tax strategy—although I have no family at home. I do encourage hiring relatives and friends as a sound introduction to the business. Recruiting your secretary can be easier than recruiting your sister.
RG: Encourage.
JPL: Setting ground rules and sticking to them enables you to hire a relative.
JL: I feel that it really depends on the kind of business and how much interest the family member has in the business. You should know his or her long-term goals for the business and what he or she will bring to the table to make it happen. It should all be put in writing so there can be no misunderstandings down the road.
AR: Encourage.
ES: I used to be death on this one. Now that we've got so much income, it's becoming more appealing because it's hard to find quality, like-minded people who are loyal and trustworthy. And there could also be tax advantages to hiring your children.

When legal issues arise, what's your usual response?
GB: I hire it out. Avoid legal problems but hire a professional.
RG: Not a good use of time.
JPL: Call my Pre-Paid Legal attorney.
JL: It really depends on what the issue is and how serious it is as to whether I try to handle it myself or not. I would review all options and if I could not resolve it myself satisfactorily, I would seek legal counsel, and turn it over to an attorney.
AR: We haven't had to deal with this.
ES: I immediately call my five-star business attorney and tell him what I want him to do. If I need a legal document such as a contract, I have found that it's best to draft a document for him to insert the "legalese" for me.

Does earning a lot of money improve the quality of your life, and if so, in what ways?
GB: Yes, it helps remove obstacles.
RG: Yes, it gives me the freedom to do what I want.
JPL: Most definitely. Time takes on a different meaning; there is more of it to do the things you always said you would do! Not having to think twice about a purchase removes stress from all areas of your life, health, vacations, charities, etc.
JL: Yes, absolutely! My husband and I have the financial and time freedom that most people want but never risk going after. We feel very blessed and it gives us the extra money to be able to help less fortunate people.
AR: We have been able to improve the quality of our life tremendously with the extra money. We have several grandchildren and have been able to help put them through college. We also help some charitable foundations.
ES: Yes, in MOST ways! While there are some things that money can't buy, I now have a life I love. I have a full-time maid, cook, landscaper, bookkeeping services, and office help. I have my first cup of coffee delivered with my newspaper in the morning and my bed turned down for me at night. I go to spas for relaxation, get weekly massages, have two gorgeous lakeside estates, go to the World Series every time my team wins, fly first class, etc..

Best general tax advice?
GB: First, invest in yourself and your business second because these have the best return on investment.
RG: Be careful.
JPL: Pay taxes on a monthly basis.
JL: Make sure you hire the best tax accountant you can afford and one that has your interest at heart. Save and file all business related expenses on a daily or weekly basis. My husband Ron, a CPA, has developed a very simplified tax record keeping system for MLMers and others in a home business called the "Be Ready Tax Record Keeping System." It makes record keeping easy and simple. Follow the simple directions and hand the whole system to your accountant at year end. If you are interested in his sys-

tem, please contact me.

AR: Get into a trust.

ES: Utilize all strategies legally available for home-based business entrepreneurs but do not even think about off-shore tax avoidance schemes. Be thankful to know that the more money you're paying, the more money you're earning. I'm proud to be an American and happy to be doing my rightful share to support schools, public services, road construction, and other necessities for our free-enterprise system.

Best general investment advice?

GB: Define your personal style and your investment objectives.

RG: Don't get too risky. Get an advisor.

JPL: Find an expert in whatever area you are investing.

JL: Make sure you know who you are and where you are going. Set goals. Write them down and read them often. Stay on track and keep focused on your goals. Take risks. That is, get out of your comfort zone and reach out. Stretch yourself. Nothing ventured, nothing gained.

AR: Find good funds.

ES: Invest in yourself -- both for self-improvement and your own business. You can control the outcome more there. Be sure you pay all taxes owed quarterly and utilize the 10% solution (save at least 10% of what you make). REMEMBER: It's not what you make that counts, but what you keep.

You're in business already, and you've just received a windfall of $20,000. What would you do with it?

GB: Invest in yourself and the business.

RG: Reduce debt, invest in yourself with personal training and coaching, buy any needed business-building tools and extra products, and invest in investments.

JPL: Depending on the stage of the business that you are in, I would invest it.

JL: God gets 10%, and who knows what I would do with the rest of it?

AR: We would donate it to charity.

ES: If I didn't have all the equipment I needed for the year and I had a genuine need for some (like a new computer or a printer), I'd buy it because you can deduct up to $18,000 off the top for large equipment purchases in tax deductions. I'd definitely bank at least $2000 of it for the 10% solution. If my company had any product promotions, I'd take advantage of those. If I had any unhappy spouse or family members, I'd definitely get them a treat off their dreams list.

NETWORK MARKETING:

What do you lead with -- your company's products or the business opportunity?

GB: Products.

RG: Usually neither. I lead with the Nutraceutical industry first.

JPL: Combination of both.

JL: Depends on the prospects's leading interest—products or opportunity. Usually, I lead with the opportunity.

AR: We lead with vision of where you might want to be in five years from now, and also the vision of where our company is going the next five years. It will be one of the biggest companies in the world.

ES: Product, usually; occasionally, lifestyle.

Rank the following traits in order of their importance in building a successful network marketing business: enthusiasm, persistence, knowledge, communication skills...

GB: Persistence, enthusiasm, communication skills, knowledge.

RG: Persistence, enthusiasm, communication skills, knowledge.

JPL: Persistence, enthusiasm, communication skills, knowledge.

JL: Enthusiasm, communication skills, persistence, knowledge.

AR: Enthusiasm, persistence, communication skills, knowledge.

ES: Enthusiasm, communication skills, persistence, knowledge.

How long were you in network marketing before you saw your first four-figure commission check? Five-figure check?

GB: Six months; 12 years.

RG: 19 years; 19.5 years

JPL: Three months; 6 months.

JL: Two months; 9 months.

AR: We were in Nikken for two years before we saw the first four-figure monthly income and three years for the five-figure monthly income.

ES: Two years; Over two years. Once I started making money, I never stopped. It only escalated.

What's more important -- the initial contact with a prospect or the follow-up?

GB: The follow up.

RG: The follow up.

JPL: Following up with a prospect says more about how important you feel your product is and that you really care about him or her.

JL: I feel that they are equal in importance.

AR: The initial contact is the most important, but if you don't follow up you might lose them. They never call you back, so you have to be sure and follow up on your new contact.

ES: Well, this is a tricky question --especially for me since I recently wrote an article for a business magazine entitled "The Magic of Follow-Up." However, the initial contact is crucial to peak their attention and get them to even look at the material or to have a belief in the program. I work my magic in the first few minutes so that I get the right ambiance going. The weaker you are in business and presentation, the more important follow-up becomes (if you ever want to convert any leads at all!).

You've just recruited a promising new distributor -- how do you help them get off to a good start -- or do you consider that the new distributor's responsibility?

GB: First I help educate and offer business support.

RG: Do a Getting Started Meeting and keep in contact every day. Help set 30- and 90-day goals. Do 3 way conference calls with them.

JPL: You are responsible for inoculating, training and helping your new recruit until you feel you can let him fly on his own.

JL: I am willing to share my success techniques with all of my new distributors, if they have an open mind and are coachable. I write articles on network marketing for the "Wealth Building" Magazine. These articles usually pull a lot of leads that I share with my new distributors that are really trying.

AR: As we recruit new distributors, we do a 2-hour training with them to find out what their goals are, getting a prospect list, etc.

ES: I personally run one of my customized Body Fitness Profiles for all new distributors so that they can take a look at the "color snapshot" of their particular body systems and get the optimum body balancing program to specifically meet their needs. They then get such great results that they are totally sold on the program I work with.

How do you get your best leads?
GB: Telephone reply to direct mail.
RG: Referrals.
JPL: Referrals and people you meet on a daily basis.
JL: Lead companies, magazine articles, newspaper ads, direct mail.
AR: The "3 Feet Rule." If they are within 3 feet of me, I tell them about it.
ES: Referrals and from my talk shows.

I'm planning a big local meeting. What's the best way to fill the room?
GB: Personal invitations and word of mouth.
RG: Have a speaker that people are eager to hear.
JPL: Contact your key players...bill a super star from another area, broadcast faxing all leaders in surrounding territories and make the event a source of recognition for all who attend.
JL: Phone calls, direct mail, personal invitations with RSVP.
ES: Newspaper coverage, radio interviews, ads, television blurbs, flyers at businesses, direct mail, and DEFINITELY a specific number of guest commitments from local distributors. Of all the things mentioned above, direct mail seems to be the least effective in my experience.

I need to generate a hundred leads within 60 days. What's my best strategy to achieve this?
GB: First, maximize the use of your personal skills.
RG: Make a list of everyone you know and ask for referrals.
JPL: In my business this would be a cooperative effort of contacting at least 20 people, asking them each for 10 people they know who would like to own their own business or who may be looking to earn additional income. You may only get one or two from each, but from those contacts you will get more leads.
JL: Newspaper ads.
AR: Our best leads are from very casual acquaintances, they listen to you more than a close friend.
ES: For me, it would be television and/or radio talk show appearances or maybe a newspaper interview. I do those things for my organization as well as for my own building.

How many distributors must a person recruit each month to succeed in network marketing?
GB: Must, zero; Should, four to eight.
RG: Until you are making $100,000 a year, at least one to four a month.

JPL: This is strictly measured by what you wish to achieve. A good rule of thumb is one new recruit per week.

JL: I feel that it's quality that counts, not quantity. Three or four people a month. Two good serious recruits should generate a sizable downline in a year or so.

AR: If you are going to be successful in network marketing you must talk to about five to ten people a week and recruit about two to three a month for the first six months. Then, you help your downline. In five and a half years, we have personally recruited (sponsored) about 38 people and have about 5,000 in our downline.

ES: It varies. Recruitment needs vary as greatly as the compensation plan structures vary. I never stop recruiting. It keeps me fresh and excited.

Best tips for surviving rejection?

GB: If everyone could do this job right then it would be worth the minimum wage. It's not easy, it does take work, and it pays according to your results. To get paid what you are worth, I recommend network marketing. But don't expect to establish an entire career within a few months.

RG: By realizing the truth—that "rejection" in this business is an illusion 99.9% of the time. Rejection is an interpretation that is not only useless and disempowering, it is invalid. If someone has a different opinion than you about the viability of your business, they are not rejecting you. If you think they are, check it out by asking them if they are rejecting you. You'll find out they are not rejecting you at all -- they just have a different opinion.

JPL: Look at rejection as a question. Most people are engrossed in their own lifestyle and habits. Introducing something new comes across as change. They don't understand completely. Follow up and follow through. Keep them on your side and you may at least be able to use them for a referral.

JL: The best way to overcome rejection is to not let it overcome you. Don't take it personally. Immediately move to the next person.

AR: Our best tip for surviving rejection is realizing they are not rejecting you, but are rejecting what you have to offer. They still like you.

ES: Become 10 feet tall and bulletproof!

Do you recommend that new distributors prospect close friends and family?

GB: Yes, because its free practice.

RG: Yes.

JPL: Prospecting close friends and family for referrals is the best place to start exposing your business.

JL: No, not until they have had some measure of success in their new venture.

AR: Only after they have had experience.

ES: No. Share products with family first and recruit your cold market. Later after your family gets good results, you might convert them to distributors.

In five years I'll be....
GB: Five times happier.
RG: Free and making a difference for 10 million people and will have written five books.
JPL: Slowing down but still working.
JL: Doing what I'm doing now. My Image Direction program will be known worldwide. I'll be known as the person who has made more people beautiful than anyone before me. I'll be extremely wealthy and so will many others whose lives I've touched along the way.
AR: Royal Diamonds.
ES: Well-known nationally for my creative franchise turnkey for medical doctors. I will have added at least another "0" to my monthly income. I'll be spending three months of the year in my newest log cabin training complex. My corporate wellness program will be underway.

In ten years I'll be...
GB: Five times happier than five years earlier.
RG: Still be free and doing whatever I want to do.
JPL: Financially Independent.
JL: Doing what God wants me to do—and that remains to be seen.
AR: Retired.
ES: Well-known internationally for my software franchise operation Forever Slim International, Inc. Corporate wellness will be a multi-million dollar reality headed toward a billion dollar reality. It would be crass to tell you how much money I am now making. I would just tell you that the more money I'm making, the more people I'm helping—and I am now helping millions of people.

What most motivates you in building your business?
GB: Seeing others wake up and take control of their own lives.
RG: Making a significant contribution for people and changing lives.
JPL: Financial Independence.
JL: People who need me. I have many God-given talents and feel a great need to share them with people who are willing to learn from me.
AR: We like to see other people succeed.
ES: The joy of service. I love what I do.

How often do you read books and/or listen to or watch tapes for improving your business skills or knowledge?
GB: Daily.
RG: Almost every day.
JPL: Daily through tapes in the car. Many old and new motivational books and tapes are on the market.

JL: Every day. I'm a "read-aholic."
AR: Every day.
ES: Every day.

The most underrated activity in business is?
GB: Making friends.
RG: Asking God to help you, connecting with people, building leaders.
JPL: Personal contact.
JL: Planting seeds.
AR: If you are not talking to people who are three feet away from you, you are not being very active.
ES: Simple discipline.

The most overrated activity in business is?
GB: Finding leaders.
RG: Getting out information.
JPL: Advertising.
JL: Hyping the opportunity.
ES: Knowledge of products and the need to understand ingredients and what's in the kit.

If I had to start my business all over again, what would I do differently?
GB: Be trainable and choose my team wisely.
RG: I would spend more time with the people I brought in, helping them succeed.
JPL: Focus more intently on recruiting.
JL: I would change very little except to reach out and touch more people.
AR: If we were to start our business over again, I would say less to more people.
ES: Nothing. For me, like Thomas Edison, every failure has taught me great insights. I wouldn't change a thing.

What was your worst business decision?
GB: I went full-time too quickly and ended up squeaking through the hard times with part-time jobs.
RG: Placing a strong business person under someone else before I understood the compensation plan and the resulting consequences.
JPL: Going into business with partners.
JL: I've been hurt at times by putting too much trust in some people. By doing this, I didn't diversify as soon as I should have.
ES: To continue to market a product whose efficacy I could no longer wholeheartedly believe in.

What was your best business decision?
GB: To be trainable and to replace attitudes with real knowledge.
RG: Going full time with Mannatech.
JPL: Making the final and firm decision that I would succeed.
JL: Not dwelling on past mistakes and moving on with a great attitude about life. Heal the past, live for the present, and dream for the future.
ES: To go full-time in MLM with my mentor and now my husband, Taylor Hegan.

What do you consider to be the main keys of your success?

GB: Persistence, personal vision, and long-term goals.

RG: Gods grace, perseverance, the big picture and communicating it to people with passion, my faith in myself and in others, and my continued personal growth.

JPL: The key to any measure of success is to go to work and do not quit!

JL: I feel that when I talk to people, I'm very sincere with them and they pick up on my sincerity. I try very hard to listen to what they want in their lives, what they are willing to do to get it, and how I can help them to obtain it. People really want to know that you care about them.

AR: The main keys to our success are being consistent, never giving up, and caring about the people that join our team.

ES: I am undaunted by failure and while magnetized by financial reward, I am unattached to whether or not people buy (and when given that free choice they almost always do buy).

What's your success philosophy?

GB: Continue to change and develop.

RG: 1. When the "why" is strong enough, the "How" takes care of itself. 2. The ultimate key is being a leader and developing other leaders. 3. There is no failure, there is only quitting. 4. The most important dynamic is perspective, your own and knowing how to shift the perspectives of others.

JPL: Trust in what you want and what you know, not in what you fear will or will not happen. People are more important than things. Money, like food and clothing are not everything, but no one can do without them. Don't lose perspective in the pursuit of any idol. Balance in all areas of your life is the key to all rewards.

JL: I feel that life is about people. It's not really about money. If you help enough people find and live their dreams, your dreams are a given. Put your business and life in God's hands and he will send you more leads than you can ever handle.

AR: You must have a good attitude to be successful.

ES: Surround yourself by great people and help other people achieve their dreams. Maintain focus, and exercise the necessary simple disciplines you've set until they become habits. Our motto is: "We build the people, the people build the business."

What about you has changed the most since finding success in business?

GB: My comfort zone has expanded.

RG: My level of gratitude, self confidence and ability to influence people (leadership) has increased.

JPL: In dealing with literally thousands of people over the years, I have found that one's biggest asset is probably one's biggest liability, myself included. I have learned that everyone has a pace but not necessarily mine. Not trying to fit everyone into a mold was a long hard lesson. My perspective of success has changed. Success is many different things to many different people. Finding out what it is an individual really wants and helping them get it through business has made my work more like a hobby.

JL: I've always been pretty successful and have lived a gifted life. So, I guess I can honestly say that the two biggest changes in my life are: 1. I now have the time freedom that once was only a dream and 2. I have a residual income that goes on and on that I didn't have before.

AR: I am happier.

ES: Adding a few zeros has allowed me to do more of the desirable service things I enjoy and it certainly gives me a "presence" that attracts the quality people I am seeking to work with. In a word: lifestyle.

What is the legacy you hope to leave?

GB: I'd like to leave behind a group of self-sufficient people who determine their own futures while building a better world.

RG: That I made God happy by loving Him and empowering millions of people, including my wife and family.

JL: I would like to be remembered as a person who was never too big or too rich to take time out to recognize a person, who was struggling with trying to better themselves. To then reach out and touch that person with enough love and attention that they would soon soar with the eagles. I feel that sometimes the world only recognizes and pays attention to the "winners." I want to be known as the person that loved them all - no matter their status.

AR: We will have helped a lot of people who can dream again, meaning they have reached their goals. That's what business is all about, helping others to help others.

ES: My legacy is to completely fulfill my mission of wellness in the world, and that includes mental, physical, emotional, spiritual and financial wellness. In this realm, I want to passionately make a difference in the lives of millions of people, and I am doing just that.

Carol Ely

Name: Carol Ely

Family: Roy (husband); Jeffrey (son), 26; Courtney (daughter-in-law), 22; Channing Alexas (granddaughter), 9 months

Highest Education: High school

Employees: None

Year Started Business: 1992

Type Of Business: New Image International specializes in diet and weight-loss products

Best Month (Gross Revenue): "No one would believe me if I told you. Network marketing has made our family financially independent. We have far exceeded our expectations."

Hours Worked Per Week During Start-Up: 70+ hours

Hours Worked Per Week Now: "40+ because I love network marketing and what I do." .

Favorite Business Magazines: Working At Home, Upline Journal, Six-Figure Income

Favorite Business Books/Authors: The Bible, What to Say When You Talk To Yourself—Shad Helmstetter, The Greatest Salesman in the World—Og Mandino

Best Thing About Being Self-Employed: Freedom to do what she wants when she wants without having to ask a BOSS if she can take time off. "It is a great feeling to decide if I want to roll out or roll over every morning without having to set an alarm clock, knowing that I can take time for my family whenever we want to. My husband has been invited to play in the Sam Snead Pro-Am Golf Tournament every year for the last four years at the Greenbrier Resort in White Sulfur Springs, West Virginia. We don't have to ask anyone if we can go. We just go, and it is one of my favorite trips each year. We go with four other couples who are in our New Image Business. The lifestyle and friendships are our greatest rewards."

Relaxes By: Reading and spending quality time with her family and friends. "There's no better relaxation than to spend quality time with the people you love and care about."

Stays Fit By: Taking New Image products. "I am in better shape than I was five years ago when we started with New Image International."

Favorite Part Of Her Business: "I love helping other people reach their goals and dreams. It is so rewarding to have a person come up to you and say 'You believed in me until I could dream again.' Now those people are duplicating and helping other people to get their dreams back. Some people have never had anyone to believe in them—not even their parents. It is a great feeling to know that you have a vehicle called network marketing that can take not only you but everyone who is willing to pay the price to financial freedom."

Least Favorite Part Of Her Business: Spending too much time with the wrong people to only find out that they are not willing to pay the price for success. "All of us at one time has had someone we thought would be a superstar. To watch that person fail is the hardest and least favorite part of our business."

Heros: Dale Calvert—"He taught me personal development was the key to success in life and everything you do. He is my mentor. One of Dale's favorite quotes is, 'People don't care how much you know until they know how much you care.' Another one is 'Ignorance is to continue to do what you have always done expecting different results. If nothing changes nothing changes.'" John Maxwell—one of the best authors on leadership. "His books have inspired me to become a better leader." Jim Rohn—"I love his tapes because 90% of his works are taken from the laws of sowing and reaping in the Bible. If you reap you must sow, and I love his challenge: 'Let others lead small lives but not you.'"

Admired Companies: Mary Kay and Amway

Special Accomplishments: Member of the Founders Club with New Image International, received the 1995 Coveted Eagle Leadership Award, consistently in the top five money earners, earned top position of the company (National Director)

Contact Carol At: (606) 528-1582

Johnny Keller

Age: 37

Family: Karen (wife), 39; Children: Nicole, 7; Joshua, 5; Lindsey, 1

Highest Education: Three years of college

Year Started Business: Started network marketing in 1980; full time since 1991

Type Of Business: Network marketing

Got In Business For Himself Because: "My father encouraged me as a young boy to go into business for myself. He told me that the only way, or the best way, to truly acquire wealth in America, was to be in business for yourself. So he planted a seed in me as a young man to think about being in business for myself. I actually started when I was a teenager, so that was very, very helpful advice he gave me."

Number Of Employees: None

Best Month (Gross Revenues): $2.3 million (wholesale)

Hours Worked per Week During Start-Up: 60 to 70 hours

Hours Worked Per Week Now: "Although I don't have to, I currently work 50 to 60 hours a week on my business. I am just so passionate about what I do, I love it so much, it doesn't even seem like work to me."

Best Thing About Being Self-Employed: "The best thing about being self-employed in network marketing is that I can help many other people achieve optimal health and financial freedom. It's a great feeling going to bed every night knowing that I've empowered other people and made a difference in their lives. It's great being able to pick and choose who you would like to work with."

Favorite Business Magazines: Network Marketing Lifestyles, Six-Figure Income, and Forbes

Favorite Business Books and Authors: The Secret Kingdom—Pat Robertson, How to Succeed at Being Yourself—Joyce Meyer, and The Greatest Networker in the World—John Milton Fogg

Relaxes By: Golfing and traveling with family and friends

Keeps In Shape Physically By: Working out six days a week and doing cardiovascular and weight training

Favorite Part Of Business: Helping others achieve their dreams and goals and watching them grow spiritually and as people

Least Favorite Part Of Business: People who are gossips and negative people that complain and moan

Admired Companies: Royal Bodycare, Amway, and Mary Kay Cosmetics

Heroes: Jesus—there was never anyone that had a more profound effect on the world than Jesus himself. "One of my favorite scriptures is, 'They will know us by our love,' and I believe that there needs to be a whole lot more love in this world. Mother and Father—"They had to overcome many obstacles. My father's father died when he was only 14, and both of my parents are hearing-impaired. Although they had many obstacles to overcome, they never quit. They always put a roof over our head and food on the table. On top of that, my father taught me the value of working hard and being honest. My mother showed me the value of loving people and accepting them unconditionally. My parents are certainly heroes of mine. I was very blessed to have parents like my mother, Marcia, and my father, John." Mr. Clinton Howard—he has achieved so much as a businessman during the course of his life, but he has done even more as a person. He really cares about helping people, he really adheres to the philosophy "It's easy to make a buck but a lot harder to make a difference." He has done so much to make a difference in so many people's lives.

Special Accomplishments: Named the #1 earning associate with Mannatech, member of the Founding Associate Advisory Council, a current member of the Associate Marketing Council, and a Platinum 22-Star Presidential Director

Favorite Quotes: "As a man thinketh in his heart, so is he."—Bible; "If you think you can, or can't, you're right."—Henry Ford; "Never, never, never, never, never quit."—Winston Churchill

Contact Johnny At: (828) 658-8141

Lance Lomako

Age: 28

Family: Single

Highest Education: High school

Year Started Business: 1995

Type Of Business: Network marketing

Market: Anyone wanting more time, income, and friends

Number Of Employees: None

Best Month (Gross Revenues): $47,000

Hours Worked Per Week During Start-Up: 20 hours per week while holding a full-time job

Hours Worked Per Week Now: 20-40 hours per week

Favorite Business Magazines: Robb Report, Success, and Upline Journal

Favorite Business Books And Authors: 21 Irrefutable laws of leadership—John C. Maxwell, Think & Grow Rich—Napolean Hill, Master Keys to Riches—Napolean Hill

Relaxes By: Playing classical guitar, painting, and exercising

Keeps In Shape Physically By: Swimming, exercising with aerobics, and studying Tai Kwondo

Favorite Part Of Business: Seeing the sparkle in someone's eyes after a presentation and knowing that they're embarking on a journey

Least Favorite Part Of Business: Seeing people's own mental roadblocks keep them from becoming successful.

Companies Admired: Microsoft and Amway

Heroes: Ivey Stokes for forging a path, blazing a trail, and lifting up so many people. His dream is big enough to encompass the world. He's a visionary and a solid role model for the community.

Special Accomplishments: Triple Crown Presidential Director and National Trainer

Favorite Quotes: If you think you can, if you think you can't, either way your right.—Henry Ford; Obstacles are what you see when you take your eyes off of your goals—Unknown

Contact Lance At: (425) 646-4368

Jim Lutes

Age: 39

Family: Single

Highest Education: High school and one year of college

Year Started In Business: 1989

Type Of Business: Nutritional network marketing

Market: Individuals seeking to create income; people who use nutrition to prevent disease, as well as those who already suffer from an ailment

Number Of Employees: One part-time employee

Best Month (Gross Revenues): $24,000

Hours Worked Per Week During Start-Up: 60 to 80 hours per week

Hours Worked Per Week Now: 30 to 40 hours per week

Best Thing About Being Self-Employed: "The challenge of making it happen, as well as not having a cap on my income."

Favorite Business Magazines: Home Business, Inc., Network Marketing Lifestyles, and Money

Favorite Business Books And Authors: The Magic of Thinking Big—David Schwartz; The Secret of Secrets—U.S. Anderson; Think and Grow Rich—Napolean Hill

Relaxes By: Riding his Harley Davidson motorcycle up the coast and meditating

Keeps In Shape Physically By: Working out regularly and practicing martial arts

Favorite Part Of Job: Putting together marketing strategies with his partners, then watching them come to fruition

Least Favorite Part Of Job: Having to understand that while the potential for success is available to all, many people just are not willing to do what is necessary to achieve it, so they never realize their true potential

Heroes: All people who overcame adversity and followed their dreams. "I have met people who will never become famous, but have faced and overcame challenges no one should endure."

Companies Admired: Integris, Dell Computer, Virgin Airlines

Favorite Quote: To change one's life, start immediately, do it flamboyantly, no exceptions.—William James

Contact Jim At: (760) 635-0969

Doug West

Age: 39

Family: Linda (wife); Krystal (daughter); Elijah (grandson)

Highest Education: Associate's degree in electronics

Year Started Business: 1984

Type Of Business: Opportunity investigating, network marketing, and home-business publishing (publisher of Healthy Times, which covers natural health products)

Market: Home business entrepreneurs

Number Of Employees: 4

Best Month (Gross Revenues): $47,000

Hours Worked Per Week During Start-Up: 100+

Hours Worked Per Week Now: 60-90

Best Thing About Being Self-Employed: "We have 300 acres here in the beautiful Kiamichi mountains of Oklahoma. This is the foot of the Ozarks. There is one stoplight in the whole county (Pushmataha). I hit a side street to avoid that stoplight most times. My wife and daughter work with me, and I don't have to leave the place unless I want to. Now when I go to a big city, as I did on a recent trip to Sacramento, Calif., I cannot wait to get back to Push County! The Internet makes it really nice. When I do go on the road, I take my laptop and can work from anywhere."

Favorite Business Magazines: Opportunity Investigator Online, Six-Figure Income, Entrepreneur

Favorite Business Books And Authors: Making Money With Classified Ads—Melvin Powers, Your First Year In Network Marketing—Mark Yarnell, SuccessfulMLM—Doug West

Relaxes By: Fishing, swimming, skiing, reading, staring at the stars and/or ocean

Keeps In Shape Physically By: Walks, push-ups, sit-ups, taking PLENTY of supplements

Favorite Part Of Job: Watching folks make more income than they've ever earned in their lives

Least Favorite Part Of Job: Dealing with complainers, whiners, and negative people

Favorite Quotes: Whatever the mind can conceive and believe, it can achieve!—by Napolean Hill

Contact Doug At: (580)298-2778

Shawn Wheeland

Age: 38

Family: Dolores (wife), 39; Traci (daughter), 8

Highest Education: New Image University

Employees: Two

Year Started Business: 1994

Type of Business: Leadership development. Teaching people with strong reasons and a burning desire how to become professionals in the network marketing industry

Market: "Hard working people with strong ethics, whose lives have brought them to the point of being sick and tired of being sick and tired—sick of debt, the boss, too much month at the end of the money. People just ready to tear up the current script and ready to write a new, much better script. People ready to make a change."

Best Month (gross revenue): "I'll put it like this: I have secured a six-figure income for the last four years whether I get out of bed or not. Most Fortune 500 CEOs probably wish they had my lifestyle. My CPA became a team player."

Hours Worked Per Week During Start-Up: 35

Hours Worked Per Week Now: 50+ "The success of others has become a habit."

Favorite Business Magazines: Upline, Success, Business Week, Six-Figure Income

Favorite Business Books/Authors: The Bible, The Seasons of Life—by Jim Rohn, Rich Dad Poor Dad—by Robert T. Kiyosaki

Relaxes By: Traveling with friends to the Caribbean, Hawaii, and Breenbrier Resort; enjoying quiet time before bed reading or planning; playing golf

Favorite Part Of His Business: "The ability to significantly influence other lives cannot be taken for granted. When I help someone see and have all there is to have in network marketing, I not only change their lives but the lives of generations to come. I'm creating change agents. Being a change maker is the best part of my business."

Least Favorite Part Of His Business: "Watching people follow those who do not have what they want. People settling for a mediocre life or trading time for money. People not living up to the challenge of growing and becoming better."

Admired Companies: Amway, Shaklee, Mary Kay—"They have proven themselves and withstood the test of time. In many ways they have pioneered this industry."

Favorite Quotes: Let others lead small lives, but not you. Let others argue over small things, but not you. Let others cry over small hurts, but not you. Let others leave their future in someone else's hands, but not you.—Jim Rohn; Adversity will teach you or defeat you. Fortunately, the choice is yours.—Shawn Wheeland; Our doubts are traitors which keep us from the good things in life by fearing to attempt.—William Shakespeare

Contact Shawn At: (803) 648-6880

The Interviews

Carol Ely
(CE)

Johnny Keller
(JK)

Lance Lomako
(JL)

Jim Lutes
(JL)

Doug West
(DW)

Shawn Wheeland
(SW)

GETTING STARTED:

I'm starting a home business next month. I have a maximum of $3,000 in start-up capital. Where should I invest it?

CE: Find yourself a good upline mentor. Our company New Image International has several packages containing product and sales aids to start your business quickly and correctly. Spend some of your capital on personal development, books, and tapes on the industry to build your belief. We suggest that everyone read The Magic of Thinking Big and Who Stole the American Dream?

JK: If someone were starting a home-based business next month and had $3,000 in start-up capital, I would suggest they invest it into network marketing. There's no other business that I know of where you can get involved in a business of your own with very little start-up capital and have such outstanding results. The upside potential of network marketing is limitless.

LL: Invest in books and tapes of a positive nature. Become knowledgeable about the industry and how to think right. Invest in brochures, applications, marketing materials, and any start-up cost associated with the business. Save the rest for overhead.

JL: If it is network marketing, I would first try all the products within reason. Then spend $100 on personal development tapes or books to assist in getting the correct mindset. Access someone with experience who can assist you in exposure of your business as cost effectively as possible using 3/4 of the remaining capital. Keep the rest in your business account for phone bills, etc.

DW: If you don't have a computer, I would start there. Kosoma can set you up with an awesome Web machine. Then I would get into some type of online business opportunity, preferably utilizing network marketing. Stay away from the tons of garbage plans that are out there. Read every issue of Opportunity Investigator Online to get ideas. We've spent many thousands investigating home business opportunities so you don't have to. You can subscribe to Opportunity Investigator Online at www.kosoma.com/subscribe.html. You can view back issues online too! I would spend the rest promoting your opportunity and for set-up fees to get started. We offer online business and recruiting systems for just $300 to $995. In my opinion, network marketing offers the most potential for the small amounts you can get started for. We offer a package that will put your offer in front of thousands, including our readers of Opportunity Investigator Online, for just a few hundred dollars. If your opportunity is not what we consider quality (and we have investigated hundreds of them), we will not take the order. This is one way to find out if you have a workable plan. For info, send an e-mail to: ttlmktpack@kosoma.com, with the subject, TOTAL-MARKETING-PACKAGE. Whatever you do, I definitely feel the Internet is the way to go. You have a much higher caliber of prospect online, and you can do business around the world! There are many excellent opportunities out there. Do your homework, use common sense, and stay away from the garbage.

SW: Find a low, start-up cost ($300 to $2,000) home-based business with proper training, a product you can believe in, a compensation plan that not only pays you but challenges you to develop others, a mother company that will do product research and development, payroll, shipping, and storage, legal issues, customer service, and all other administrative aspects of a traditional business. Delve into the systems that had been time tested and time proven and don't analyze every five minutes. Rock and roll and don't look back. Just Do It!

I've just started a home business. My spouse has given me six months to make it work. Any advice?

CE: I can deal with skeptical spouses because we have cassette tapes and satellite training to deal with this. Negative people, even if it is your spouse, will do everything to see that you do not succeed. When I started my business, my husband gave me one month to pay off the credit card with which I charged the products and tools. I sold all my product and paid it off in one week, plus I had over $750.00 in profit from my sales to re-invest back into my business. My spouse was never negative, just skeptical, until he saw that network marketing was our key to the American Dream.

JK: It takes awhile to develop a business, and I would simply ask for a little bit more time and produce results. Because success is relative; the more success, the more relatives.

LL: Start by educating your spouse about business prosperity and that to become a success in any venture, it takes a commitment of at least three to five years. But after that, the two of you can own the rest of your lives and raise your children the way you want to.

JL: Honestly, if your spouse is setting conditions on your success from day one, then I would reconsider starting a business at all. It may take some individuals four months just to acquire the skills to be self-employed and run a business.

DW: Ask your spouse where you or they will be in six months if you just keep working a job. You might very well be successful in six months, but what if it takes a year or two? No reason to give up on the idea of your own business. Most small businesses fail within a couple of years. With a home business you have more staying power and fewer expenses. The longer you stay in business, the more chance you are giving yourself to succeed.

SW: Ask him or her for help so together you can create 12 months of productivity in six months. Tell them that if they are unwilling to help you pursue your dream, you need a year. By the way, never get involved in any opportunity that requires that you give up your current cash flow (job/business) until you have first replaced that cash flow.

They say it takes money to make money. Should I try to get a small business loan for my start-up capital or just try to get by with my own limited finances?

CE: I would never suggest anyone get a loan. If you can not afford $500 or so to get into business, then you are financially in jail. I ask everyone who says they can not afford $500 to start a business if they were to get in jail through no fault of their own how would they come up with the $500 to get out of jail? It never fails, they suddenly remember where to get the money. At New Image International, we teach people with limited funds to set aside their retail profits. Pay 10% to their church, 15% on themselves and the rest into their business until they have built a solid residual income.

JK: If you are going to get a business loan for start-up capital, make sure that you have a good business plan in place. Make sure that you have a system that greatly increases the chance of your succeeding. If you do not, then I would just try to get by with limited finances until I found someone that could mentor me and help make my chance for success in network marketing a whole lot better.

LL: I started out with almost no financial backing and living paycheck to paycheck, but in my business sweat equity alone can build a lifetime of income.

JL: This business is built through labor and investment and various combinations of both. The more you wisely invest in the exposure of your company (not in joining the company!) the faster your business will grow. So it's up to the individual and where their risk tolerance is.

DW: I personally would stay away from any loans if you can help it. Find a GREAT NETWORK MARKETING plan that you can get started with for just a few hundred. If you have to, borrow that from a friend or relative. Once you pay them back, sign them up!

SW: Start where you are at. Our business is best performed by people who are value focused. Starting in debt and having to make the money will create a survival focus putting you at a great disadvantage. If the opportunity is real, you can start anywhere and explode to the top. All a successful person needs is an opportunity.

Do you consider yourself an "early adopter" of new technology?

CE: Yes, I love to learn and teach others, but the most important thing is not to lose touch with personal relationships. That is the key to network marketing—keeping in touch and being a mentor.

JK: I do not consider myself an early adopter of new technology. I usually like to wait until it's on the market for a little while. Usually new technology is very expensive, and if you wait a little the prices drop dramatically. I want to make sure that that new technology does indeed work.

LL: Not exactly. I just acquired a computer a few months ago.

JL: No, not at all.

SW: Yes.

If you use a toll-free phone number, what is the primary use for your toll-free line?

CE: Lead generation.

JK: The primary use for my toll-free line is to use it in advertising to acquire more customers and business builders for my networking business.

JL: National ads.

DW: Orders only.

SW: Advertising and organization support.

Technology Utilized

	Fax*	Fax-on-Demand	Toll-Free	Voice Mail	Computer	Email	Internet	Website	Email Auto-Responders
Carol Ely	✓	✓	✓	✓	✓	✓	✓	✓	✓
Johnny Keller	✓	✓	✓	✓	✓	✓	✓	✓	✓
Lance Lomako	✓	✓		✓	✓	✓	✓		
Jim Lutes	✓	✓	✓	✓	✓	✓	✓		
Doug West	✓	✓	✓	✓	✓	✓	✓	✓	✓
Shawn Wheeland	✓	✓	✓	✓	✓	✓	✓	✓	✓

* Dedicated fax line

What is your computer system?

CE: An IBM, 266 MHz system with a 20-inch screen. I also have a Hewlett Packard DeskJet 870Cse printer and a Hewlett Packard flatbed scanner, a plain paper Brother fax machine, and a Cannon personal copier.

LL: I am somewhat illiterate when it comes to computers, but primarily I use it to send and receive mail, communicate, and do research.

JL: Simple laptop for writing letters, etc.

DW: Several PC's, scanners, a digital camera, Zip drives, and printers. We use it all!

SW: A 233 MHz Power Mac and a Power Mac 3400c, a scanner, and a Zip drive for backing up data.

What software do you consider in the "must-have" category?

CE: Microsoft Works and Microsoft Office Suite, Lotus Smart Suite and Quicken for bookkeeping.

LL: Word, Windows.

JL: Basic business software.

DW: Netscape Communicator. We teach folks how to master their business with it. From Web design to e-mail management, we think it is the most underrated FREE program on the net! NOTEMAID is also a nice little plain text editor we use daily. Of course, you have to have some type of word processor and a good FTP program.

SW: Microsoft Office, QuickBooks, Adobe Photoshop, Now Up-To-Date and Contact.

What other technologies, if any, do you use in your business?

CE: Cellular phone.

JK: Cell phone, laptop computer.

LL: Cell phone, and conference calls.

JL: Cell phone.

DW: Laptop computer, Follow-Up Responders

SW: Cell phone, E-organizer, scanner

Name up to five personal favorite business URL's our readers can benefit from:

CE: www.mlmhelp.com, www.newimageint.com, www.upline.com, www.mlmers.com, www.mlm.com.

LL: mlm.com, Anywho.com, nasdaq.com.

DW: www.kosoma.com, www.kosoma.com/subscribe.html, youonline.net, kosoma.com/FreeAdLinks.html, www.efax.com.

SW: www.mlmhelp.net, www.mlmhelp.com, www.homebusiness.com, www.sixfigureincome.com, www.monster.com.

Of all the technology you use, rank your top three:

CE: Phone, computer, voice mail.

JK: Internet, voice mail, cell phone.

LL: Phone, voice mail, computer.

JL: Cell phone, 800 number, corporate Website.

DW: The Internet, computers, the World Wide Web

SW: Cell phone, computer, e-organizer.

Do you market on the Internet?

CE: Yes, to generate leads, we give our Website and www.mlmhelp.com to new leads to check out our story along with the story of our company and Director of Marketing, Dale Calvert. Dale has a newsletter that I suggest to every lead I talk with personally (who has an e-mail address) to go read. I want them to read the articles and call me back with any questions. We sell product also from our Web page.

JK: Yes. I have my own Website and we have just developed a marketing campaign through the Internet, which will generate thousands of leads.

LL: No.

JL: I will be.

DW: Yes, we utilize e-mail marketing, contests, links, an affiliate program, banners, and e-zines.

SW: Yes, for lead generation.

Approximately what % of your sales originate from this marketing?

CE: About 15% or more.

JK: Too early to tell.

DW: 90%.

SW: 10%.

Do you use direct mail?

CE: Yes. This is a warm-market business. We only run ads in the cold market to support our future leaders in that area. We never go to a city unless leadership takes us there. Then we run ads to support this leader. We have customized recruiting programs that we use in local markets throughout the United States and Canada. Some of our programs are for ministries, stay-at-home mothers, chiropractors, and small-business owners. We have cassettes to support these programs.

JK: Yes, we use direct mail to acquire members by sending out a lead audiotape. We also use direct mail to bond our customers to us and our products.

LL: No.

JL: Yes, to generate consumer sales.

DW: Less and less all the time, though that is how I started. We still use post cards and printed issues of Opportunity Investigator Online.

SW: Yes, we print and mail letters and flyers.

Approximately what % of your sales originate from this marketing?
CE: About 20% of our leads come from the print media.
JL: 50%.
DW: 2%.
SW: 7%.

Do you use print media (e.g. magazines, newspapers, card decks)?
JK: Yes, I use these forms of advertising to find other business builders.
JL: Yes, to generate and establish customer bases.
DW: Yes, sometimes we use card decks to drive people to our Website.
SW: Yes, we use card decks. We also run ads in newspapers and magazines.

Approximately what % of your sales originate from this marketing?
JK: I would say approximately 25% of our sales generate from this form of marketing.
JL: 50%.
DW: 1%.
SW: 5%.

Do you use radio and/or TV advertising?
CE: Yes. New Image International has a powerful 30-minute infomercial that we run in our future leaders' local markets to generate leads for both our products and the business opportunity. The TV show allows me and our leaders to focus in on a specific city where we have an up-and-coming leader. We run the TV shows, work the leads, and build one solid line under our up-and-coming leader while supporting them with their warm market.
JK: We have used both radio and TV advertising to recruit new members.
LL: No.
JL: Yes, radio, to establish customer bases.
DW: We recently had ads running on ZDTV, the TV network that covers nothing but the Internet.
SW: We have used TV (company supported infomercial).

Approximately what % of your sales originate from this marketing?
CE: This generates approximately 25% of our leads.
JK: A very small percentage.
JL: 50%.
DW: 5% to 7%. We will be doing more TV ads in the future, all designed to drive folks to our Website.
SW: 2%.

What other kinds of marketing do you utilize?
CE: If you ask any of our distributors that joined our company, you will find out that 80% or more came from our system and call-back service. They were satisfied cus-

tomers first and backed into our business because we have a system that works if they work. We do product brochures, drop cards, car signs, bumper stickers, mini-billboards, car sun shades, bulletin board tear-off flyers, trade shows, fairs, buttons ("Lose weight now, Ask me How"). We teach specific step-by-step methods for all our retail activities. New Image International's philosophy is you retail to recruit.

JK: There are many forms of marketing that we utilize. We have been especially successful in generating business through our tape-mailing program. We spent a lot of time and money testing different lists. We have a proven system that works as far as tape mailing is concerned. We know approximately what percentage of people respond, what percentage of those people will actually sign up into our business, and what the initial average first order is. We also know what the reorder rate will be. So this has been very, very successful for us, and it is our primary form of marketing.

LL: Word of mouth, warm market, video tapes, home party presentations, and teleconferencing.

JL: Newspaper and local media.

SW: Warm market systems.

Do you recommend using a toll-free number in advertising? Why or why not?

CE: I recommend it if I am doing the advertising, but not for a new distributor. We want that new person's phone to ring off the hook. I only use my toll-free number for nationwide advertising. On this voice mail box I have my local number where I can be reached—the serious ones will call you personally, the other 80% we don't want. I have found that in cold-market advertising, 80% are just curious but not seriously looking for an opportunity.

JK: I absolutely recommend using a toll-free number in advertising. It has been shown time and time again to greatly increase the amount of your response.

LL: If I were to advertise on a national basis, I would use a toll- free number.

JL: On a national basis, yes, unless affordability is a problem.

DW: I've heard pros and cons. Rates are getting so cheap now, why not?

SW: Yes, but not always. Numbers (ratios) don't lie. More calls come for ads with toll-free numbers.

Where do you market?

CE: In the United States and Canada.

JK: I market locally, nationally, and internationally now because of the Internet.

LL: United States.

JL: Locally, nationally, and internationally.

DW: Nationally and internationally.

SW: Locally, nationally, and internationally.

How should someone set up their home office to maximize its effectiveness?

CE: The quietest place with as much privacy as you can find. I started in my dining room and later moved to my formal living room because we never used it. Now it is the most active room in our home.

JK: My best recommendation on someone setting up a home office is to go actually visit some people who have their own home office. Ask them what they feel is best about their home office, and if they made any mistakes, what they were. It would be best to find somebody that has already been established for years and has refined and honed their home office to make it as effective as possible. If you do not have someone that you can meet with at their home office, I would recommend you buy a book on setting up a home office. There are many out there that will help you along the way.

LL: I believe in the Chinese art of Feng Shui. It is the art of setting up your home as an effective use of space to help the creative energy flow and fun, expanded living. I think the office should be in a place that you feel very comfortable spending your time. Keep it neat and clean with plenty of good lighting and a chair with ample back support.

JL: The important thing is to delegate an area for your office, because if you have never been in business before, this business is easily out-of-sight, out–of-mind.

DW: Hopefully you will start out with an organized office. I have had to improvise as the business grew. Now it seems we are expanding all the time.

SW: Others must live in your house, so establish the communication center (office) in a room away from noise and distractions, but close to the kitchen and bathroom. You must be able to enjoy working from home. Design a non-traditional work space. The five foot desk and high back chair is corporate and suggests the opposite of a home-based business. Put a day bed in your office and a Lazy Boy. Put pictures up that remind you why you are working (goal board). A lot of windows (area open to the outside) represents freedom.

Are there any ground rules you've established for yourself, family, etc. for operating at home successfully?

CE: Our son was in college when I started our business. He and my husband have always been supportive of me, so I never had to have any rules established. They know when I am in my office, I am working and they don't interrupt unless it is important.

JK: The ground rules that we have established for our family for operating at home successfully are: We put God first, we put the family second, and we put the business third. Also, we recognize that when I am working, it is work time and when I am with my family, it is family time. So we have the ability to separate the two, even though I have a home-based business. I have worked from both my home and an office, and I have found that I am more effective working at home because it's a much more pleasant surrounding and it allows me to have a very short commute. My commute is only 30 seconds, and that's much better than half an hour or an hour. So it actually frees up more time for me, thus allowing me to be more productive.

JL: Total discipline. Work time is work time. No TV while you're working or any other distractions.

DW: When we work, we work. We have offices separate from the home. Some offices (where I work mostly) are attached to the house, but are in a separate room.

SW: Yes, when we are on the phone, no noise. Washer and dishwasher run during non-business hours. Work when it's time to work. Take breaks several times a day and have a blast!

Do you consider working at home an advantage or disadvantage to your business overall?

CE: A great big advantage, I love getting up when I want and walking 35 feet down the hallway into my office. I was a housewife and I really enjoy my freedom. A home office gives you freedom; you are in control of your destiny, not someone else.

JK: Working at home is a definite overall advantage. There are many fringe benefits of working at home. My wife is an excellent cook; I love being at home with my children because I can go ahead and take them to the park any time I want. It is my goal to see many more moms and dads at home with their children and at the park during the day. I love being at home with my wonderful wife and family.

LL: Advantage—tax benefits, traffic commute, comfortable environment.

JL: For me, a total advantage. For others, too much distraction.

DW: Advantage. No other way to do it for the small guy. In a recent trip to San Francisco I was enjoying the view as I was attempting to get on the Bay Bridge. I could enjoy it because I was just visiting. I could not help but feel for all those folks who have to put up with that traffic everyday! That's not living, folks! Why not enjoy a simple commute to your home office?

SW: Major advantage. I get paid what I am worth, instead of what a boss says I'm worth.

Do you farm out any of your work?

CE: Yes, as much as possible. I delegate everything that I can to my key leaders and upcoming leaders. I want to concentrate on developing relationships with our leaders. If you can find and develop two good leaders a year in this industry you will be a complete success.

JK: Yes. I don't have time to type, so I have found an excellent business that will do my typing for me. I would suggest that you farm out anything that you don't like to do, and that you can pay someone else to do in a reasonable fashion.

LL: No.

JL: No.

DW: I farm out printing, tech support for our customers, etc. When it comes to the money however, handle that in house!

SW: Yes. Printing, computer data input, legal work, CPA work.

Do you encourage or discourage...partnerships?

CE: Definitely discourage. I have seen so many good friendships end and families torn apart because of partnerships.

JK: I encourage partnerships. Network marketing is a business of relationships and partnerships, and it's as J. Paul Getty said, "I'd rather have 1% of 100 people's efforts than 100% of my own." We can all accomplish a lot more working together.

LL: I think the best type of partnerships are those that are husband-and-wife related. I recommend teaming up to accomplish the goals at hand, assigning specific duties. I also feel that a family working together in a synergistic atmosphere can really be a powerful driving force.

JL: Discourage if you are self motivated.

DW: Discourage.

SW: Discourage—a leader must lead. Organizations are built by leadership. Leadership is the highest paid profession in the world!

Do you encourage or discourage...hiring family members?

CE: Encourage. Our son works with me; he has saved me so much time. Not only that, but to know that you can trust who you are working with means everything in our business.

JK: I would hire family members. I have a particularly hard-working family.

JL: Discourage, even though there are tax advantages. It's a personal choice.

DW: ENCOURAGE—many tax benefits. Make those young ones work for their money! Also, no workers comp with family!

SW: That depends on the relationship.

When legal issues arise, what's your usual response?

CE: At New Image International we have a great staff that works with attorneys so we do not have to get involved. We hand over our information to the compliance department; they handle our legal issues and if they need the attention of our attorneys, we leave that up to them.

JK: My usual response is, "How can we resolve the challenge without it going to court?" The only people I believe that win when legal issues arise are the attorneys. If you can settle it out of court, not only will you save yourself a lot of time, you will also more than likely save yourself a lot of money. I do realize that sometimes it needs to go to court; however, my best advice is: if you can avoid it, at all costs definitely do so.

LL: For me, all legal issues are basically handled by corporate at the network marketing company I work with.

JL: Handle it professionally.

DW: I have had a Pre-Paid Legal membership for years, and I still get checks from them for marketing it years ago (we still sell an occasional membership from our Website). PPL has saved me more than once when legal issues arise.

SW: Handle it now!

Does earning a lot of money improve the quality of your life, and if so, in what ways?

CE: Yes, we are totally financially free, everyone should have the privilege of knowing the joy of that comes from helping others. I had heard all my life that money is the root of all evil but that is not true; it actually says the love of money is the root of all evil. When you have money, it makes you more of what you already are. If you are a giver, you will give more. If you can't handle what you have now, you will not be able to handle large sums of money. When our son got married last year we had a 2,700-square-foot home built for him and his new wife. When he got out of college we gave him a BMW Z3 Roadster. All his friends are wanting to know if I will adopt them because we only have one son! Roy (my husband) has played golf in Hawaii, Jamaica, St. Thomas, Cancun, and Aruba. These are the qualities of life that give you great memories. I tell everyone we walk the beaches of the world and New Image International is paying for it.

JK: Earning a lot of money definitely improves the quality of one's life. I've been rich and I've been poor, and being rich is a lot better because when I was poor, I could not give to charity. I could not help out starving children. I could not give money to my church. I could not be a blessing to others. Money is not the root of all evil, the love of money is the root of all evil. So you can definitely help to not only improve the quality of your own life but also improve the quality of the lives of many around you. For those of us that have been blessed financially with a lot of money, it is our obligation to help out those less fortunate than us.

LL: One word: freedom. Freedom to wake up when I want to, not being bound by a bank account. When I go on vacation now, it's not where I can afford to go, it's where I want to go. When I go shopping, I buy what I want without looking at a price tag. I have peace of mind, security, and a stress-free life.

JL: Yes, you now have less worry and more choices.

DW: Yes, as long as you don't let it go to your head. Most of the time, more is demanded of you (especially in network marketing). You have to deal with more folks, and some of them who are very negative can get pretty nasty with you. It all comes with the territory. It does give you more time to spend with your family. Especially if you all work together.

SW: Yes. First, I spend many valuable hours with my daughter. She is learning exactly what I believe. We are becoming great friends as she grows. Strangers are not raising my child. Second, when a person leverages time and gets man hours working for them, life takes on a different dimension. Life is as it should be. Lived by the person for the person, not for someone else.

Best general tax advice?

CE: Get a good CPA, one that will work with you and knows the home-business laws. If you have to tell him about a tax change, get another tax advisor.

JK: My best tax advice would be to keep accurate records and get yourself the best CPA or tax attorney that you can.

LL: Surround yourself with the best possible tax consultants.

JL: Keep separate accounts, log everything, and delegate to a good accountant who is familiar with home businesses.

DW: Get a good CPA and/or a good tax program and keep good records.

SW: Start a home-based business! Charles Givens wrote in "Wealth Without Risk," that the number one tax edge in America is a home-based business.

Best general investment advice?
CE: I feel this is so personal and different for each individual that we should only consult with an expert in this field.

JK: My best general investment advice would be, again, to get a good financial planner, preferably someone that follows the market very closely. I prefer someone that is a certified financial planner.

LL: Buy low, sell high. Use common sense, don't get into something you don't understand.

JL: Invest everything back into your business, but keep 25 to 35% separate for taxes.

DW: Don't listen to brokers! If you don't have much to play with, a good home business should be where you start. Treat it like a business, and it will pay you like one, maybe even better!

SW: Get professional help.

You're in business already, and you've just received a windfall of $20,000. What would you do with it?
CE: Give $10,000 to our church for a building project and put the rest in investment accounts for our son's family.

JK: If I had just received an unexpected windfall of $20,000, I would immediately give away at least $2,000 of it. I would take the other $18,000 and invest part of it back into my business. I would put part of it into savings.

LL: Use it to pay off debts, invest back into your own business, invest in the stock market.

JL: If my business was already profitable, I would roll it into other investment vehicles. If business was slow, exposure, exposure, exposure!!!

DW: I would promote with half of it and perhaps use some as incentives for my team to perform. I'd save the other half. I do play the market some, so my savings might well be in a mutual fund or stock.

SW: Get out of debt. No man should owe any man. Put 70% toward bills, invest 10%, give away 10% (benevolent goals), and spend 10% freely.

What do you lead with: your company's products or the business opportunity?
CE: Both. Our company, New Image International, has a proven duplicable system for doing it both ways. Our goal with our system in retailing is to sell a bottle of product, get 10 referrals, sell to five of those referrals and back that person into the business with five retail customers for them. We lead with our TV show for the business and do three-way calls with our people. We also have several cassette tapes we can lead with for the

business and product.

JK: I lead with our company's outstanding products. There's a very good reason for doing this. We have a great lead audiotape that really piques people's interest. The tape tells the same story time and time again, and it is a very duplicatable process. Now, when people become interested in trying our product, I will definitely mention to them that there is a business opportunity involved. However, in order to effectively draw in more business builders, take the pressure off. Play it cool. Make sure you don't over-pressure anyone to become a business builder. Some people just start out as customers, and that's great. We want many, many customers. What you will find is that some of your best customers become some of your best business builders. So we do indeed lead with our company's products. However, we do mention that there is a business opportunity involved, we recruit that way, and we find it's a very effective way to recruit. The proof is in the printout and we have some very large printouts.

LL: Business opportunity. I teach people to put their CEO hat on by getting into a distribution mentality. Products are extremely important, but if you're the only one on your team selling them, good luck.

JL: I target each market separately depending on their need.

DW: Business opportunity. There are more folks who want to make money than there are who are just thrilled about products. Products and/or services have to be quality, but I'm looking for business builders.

SW: Product. The best associates are first satisfied customers.

Rank the following traits in order of their importance in building a successful network marketing business: enthusiasm, persistence, knowledge, communication skills:

CE: Persistence, communication skills, enthusiasm, and knowledge.

JK: I would put enthusiasm first, persistence second, knowledge third, and communication skills fourth. The reason I say this is I have many new people that on sheer enthusiasm alone are bringing in tons of people in the business, and we know from study after study that it's not what you say but how you say it. Body language and tonality in communication is actually more an important form of communication than what you are saying. Also, I rank persistence second because it is extremely important in that there are only certain ways that you can fail, and one of them is by quitting. I've seen so many people in the network marketing industry quit right before they were going to reap a financial blessing that would absolutely make a big difference in their life. For instance, all three of the people upline from me quit, and they quit after just three months. Now, I am sure they wish that they hadn't quit and were still in the business. The #1 reason why I see people fail is because of a lack of persistence. Finally, knowledge comes from actually doing it. You can't teach what you don't do.

LL: Enthusiasm, persistence, communication skills, knowledge.

JL: Enthusiasm, persistence, knowledge, communication skills.

DW: Enthusiasm is number one (staying positive, that really is #1), followed by persistence and knowledge (I've seen enthusiastic, positive folks win out over the ones who knew it all many times. It does help to have some knowledge, though). Fourth is communication skills (a positive attitude and enthusiasm can even overcome lack of communication skills).

SW: "Nothing great was ever achieved without enthusiasm, persistence, communication skills, and knowledge.

How long were you in network marketing before you saw your first four-figure commission check? Five-figure check?

CE: 18 months, 5 months.

JK: I was in network marketing for six years before I saw my first four-figure commission check and twelve years before I saw my first five-figure income check.

LL: Six months to hit $1,200, three years to achieve $12,000.

JL: Eight months for four figures, five figures in 18 months.

DW: 10 years for four figures, five figures—almost there.

SW: Six months for four figures, 26 months for five figures.

What's more important: the initial contact with a prospect or the follow-up?

CE: Follow-up, follow-up, follow-up! If you don't follow-up, what good was the contact? Follow-up is more important than the initial contact!

JK: The fortune is in the follow-up, so I would rank the follow-up even more important than the initial contact. A lot of people on initial contact may say no, but don't take that as a final no; take it as a "not yet." I have found that many people, including some of my very top business builders said no at first. It took me many times contacting them and building a relationship before they became involved with my business. So, the follow-up is extremely important. It's a big difference in what separates amateurs from professionals. The professionals will always make sure that the follow-up is not only effective but also it shows you are a professional.

LL: Without the contact there would be no follow-up. However, both are very vital to building a large organization.

JL: Follow-up.

DW: Follow-up.

SW: Proper follow-up is always more important than the initial contact.

You've just recruited a promising new distributor. How do you help them get off to a good start. Or do you consider that the new distributor's responsibility?

CE: We do what we call a 72-hour action plan, blitz their warm market, stay with them the first 90-days. Within this time frame, it is our goal to get them a check for $500 per month. Our New Image University keeps them on target to reach the top with our company. We feel it is our responsibility for them to see success in their first 90 days and we take our responsibility serious. So many times, we do three-way calls with prospects that loved the concept of network marketing but failed because they had no direction their first 90 days. I tell every one of them it is not their fault they failed. You must have a specific step-by-step, word-by-word, unified system to take potential leaders down the road to success.

JK: When I have just recruited a promising new distributor, I help them get off to a good start by setting up a business plan. I simply ask them seven key questions, and from their response to those seven key questions I can build them a plan based upon their goals. I am a very hands-on mentor. I will jump in the trenches with anyone. I do a lot of three-way calls initially to train people how to do the business properly. I have found that three-way calling is one of the greatest assets that we have in network marketing. However, you eventually have to let the eagles fly from the nest.

LL: Teach new distributor fundamentals on how to get started working their warm market and to show them how to build properly. Take a new distributor through a turnkey training system.

JL: Put in place simple, yet mandatory tasks so they can begin to develop good habits. Do not take them to sophomore until they have finished freshman.

DW: We provide leads, a track to run on, a plan, and a "Pro Pack" from Kosoma.

SW: Everyone enters this business with the skill level to fail. I help them get off to a good start by sponsoring them, taking them under my wing, guiding, supporting, and coaching them through the New Image University.

How do you get your best leads?

CE: From the warm market of the new distributor list, we have everyone list 100 names of people they know over the age of 18. We ask them not to pre-judge any one of them and every time—it never fails—we will find three to five good potential leaders from that list.

JK: We get our best leads from doing audiotape mailings and passing out audiotapes on a local basis.

LL: I think your best leads come from what I call a chicken list—the people you know that you're afraid to contact because of their success.

JL: Warm market of new distributors and local ads.

DW: The Internet.

SW: Warm market systems.

I'm planning a big local meeting. What's the best way to fill the room?

CE: Leadership in any town in which we have meetings will fill our rooms. If you build for the event, it will take care of itself. Everything rises and falls on your local leadership. Leadership is the key to a great successful meeting.

JK: If you're planning a big local meeting, the best way to fill the room is to make sure that you're strong in that area, that the meeting is well advertised in advance, that there are very dynamic speakers, there is an incentive for people to come to the meeting, and that you do a lot of advertising for prospects and inviting people from the warm market.

LL: Have everyone in your downline bring guests.

JL: Divide the meeting into products and business. These are two different markets. Then have all local distributors build in advance—10 guests each for each category. Co-op ads may be used for this.

DW: Don't do it. Look for an Internet business opportunity where you don't have to have meetings. Most of us don't like them anyway.

SW: Never build until you have leadership. Then blitz their warm market while supporting with cold market programs.

I need to generate a hundred leads within 60 days. What's my best strategy to achieve this?

CE: Our company's infomercial. I also would run a classified ad in a nationwide paper offering our newest cassette by Dale Calvert. This cassette has been a tremendous lead generator for us.

JK: I've actually had people generate hundreds of leads within one month. The best strategy, I believe, to achieve this is to do direct mail with a very, very, very good lead tape. I've actually had someone sign up 187 people using this strategy in just one month! So if you need to generate hundreds of leads within 60 days, I would highly suggest doing a tape mailing program.

LL: Write down a list of everyone you know of. Use the yellow pages as an index to help spur your memory of people you know in all career fields.

DW: A BestAd from Kosoma (I don't know of anywhere else you can get a 100 quality leads for that price!).

SW: Warm market systems.

How many distributors must a person recruit each month to succeed in network marketing?

CE: Five a month. We teach everyone to sponsor five a month, and you can control your destiny. When you teach those five to sponsor five a month, it's like a snowball rolling downhill. You can't be stopped; success is yours.

JK: The issue is not how many people someone must recruit each month to succeed in network marketing. I'm of the firm belief it is not the quantity but the quality. It is what you do with the new recruit once you recruit them into your business. The #1 complaint I've had in my two decades of network marketing is that people are not receiving support from the upline. We teach the importance of giving not only great support, but teaching the new person the proper things that need to be done in order to achieve success. Certainly the #1 thing is self-development. This is a business of personal growth and stepping out of your comfort zone. If one does self-development initially from the beginning, not only are they much more likely to succeed, they also will be more persistent and not quit on you. Also, they will have a much better attitude.

LL: It's not a solo sport, it's a team sport. Team means Together Everyone Achieves More. It's not how many you can recruit, it's what your team can do. And every marketing plan is different as well as the definition of success.

DW: One will work; two will EXPLODE your business, if you teach others to do the same.

SW: To thrive in network marketing, you must develop the skills to recruit five a month and then teach that to others.

Best tips for surviving rejection?

CE: Most people are going to stay in their comfort zones because they don't want the fear of rejection and failure. Every time I looked at my reasons for doing network marketing, those reasons drove me to let rejection be more of a motivator than a fear. If you know WHY you are doing the business, you will survive rejection. One of Dale Calvert's favorite sayings is, "Until you know why, the how doesn't matter! Best tip I can give you is: if you don't have a 20 Reasons "Why List," go do one now.

JK: My best tip for surviving rejection is that the person isn't personally rejecting you, they're just saying "Not yet." I always felt sorry for people that said absolutely no way will I ever get involved with network marketing. Being a former financial planner, I know that only 5% of the people when they retire actually achieve financial independence. That means that 95% of the people out there are retiring broke. When they say no to me, I look at them and feel sympathy for them. Statistics show that they are going to wind up in the 95% unless they have some sort of plan. Network marketing is by far the best way to achieve financial independence in the United States and all over the world.

LL: Develop a rhino skin because rejection is a way of life for networkers. I say change your mindset. They're not rejecting you, only the opportunity at this time.

JL: Realize that most people do not want to do this. That is why YOU are doing this because you do not want to be like most people...do you?.

DW: Don't beg. Ask, "Can I get back with you in a few months to see if you have changed your mind?"

SW: Develop belief in your company, the industry, your products, and yourself. Never take advice from people who do not have what you want.

Do you recommend that new distributors prospect close friends and family?

CE: Yes, this is a warm-market business. If you found a gold mine full of gold and you needed someone to help you get the gold out of the mine, who would you call— strangers or friends and family? I believe network marketing is a gold mine. My obligation is to expose them to this industry. If they join, that's great. If they don't I just say "Next!" Some will, some won't, so what? Someone's waiting!!! Next!

JK: I absolutely recommend that new distributors prospect close friends and family. I would also recommend that it is done by a three-way call. Because they have close friends and family, there is a certain amount of trust that is built up as a result. Even though there might not be a whole lot of respect, the trust is there. The new distributor can edify the person that's doing the three-way call with them. There will be immediate respect there because of the trust that the new distributor has when prospecting their close friends and family.

LL: Absolutely! Most people would love to build their futures with family and friends. Just make sure that someone they don't know does the presentation. Get a third party to do the presentation.

JL: Yes, but not alone.

DW: Yes! In our group, they may do that AFTER they work the Internet for awhile, but why not give your family a prime position on your team?

SW: Yes, only when shown how. If you believe in your company, the products and the industry, why would you not want to excite and/or bless the ones you love the most?

THE ROAD AHEAD:

In five years I'll be....

CE: Doing what I love most in life: teaching other people that the American dream is still alive and walking the beaches of the world with my New Image family.

JK: In five years I will be in God's perfect will. I will also be doing a lot of charity work, especially the feeding of the hungry. I will be spending even more time with my family. I will be traveling the world supporting my organization, which will be 250,000+ members strong. I will continue to learn more and improve in my profession.

I will definitely be playing more golf. And finally, I will be enjoying the residual income from the network marketing business that I have built.

LL: Building my business on a global basis and changing more peoples lives financially and spiritually.

JL: Still building a business.

DW: Still avoiding traffic, making money from home (may work less though).

SW: I will be in a better position to help many more people establish a life, free from the traditional stress and fatigue associated with traditional way to make a living. I will have more true friends and relations associated with life giving, life lasting memories of the journey.

In ten years I'll be...

CE: In ten years I will be part of the most exciting organization in network marketing. We introduced the first and only training program of its kind called New Image University. Its success has far exceeded its own author's, Dale Calvert, wildest dreams. His leadership team will go down in history as the greatest group of leaders that re-wrote network marketing. We took this industry back to the grass roots, city by city, county by county, state by state, country by country, one NIU Course at a time.

JK: In ten years I will be doing everything in my five-year projection. Plus, I will be three years away from getting onto the Senior PGA Tour.

LL: Helping unify the world governments to one positive political system through network marketing.

JL: Diversified in business outside the industry and traveling.

DW: Still avoiding traffic, making money from home (may work less though).

SW: Double that of the five-year benchmark. Now I can travel the world and never stay in a hotel. I will have more peace knowing that my work has touched not only my immediate contact but their children as well. I have truly developed "Change Makers" throughout the world. These people will make a real difference.

What most motivates you in building your business?

CE: Helping and serving other people, I feel we were put here to serve. I want everyone I meet or come in contact with to know the real joy of having freedom!

JK: The thing that really motivates me in building my network marketing business is helping others achieve optimal health and financial security. It is also thrilling to watch them grow as individuals.

LL: Giving back something to people who believe in me enough to come with me on my journey to help change the world for the better.

JL: The challenge.

DW: I love helping folks make money from home!

SW: Developing "change makers" Seeing people take control of their lives.

How often do you read books and/or listen to or watch tapes for improving your business skills or knowledge?

CE: Daily. I was taught by my mentor, Dale Calvert, do something every day to improve yourself and your business. I love to read and my car is a rolling university on cassettes.

JK: I read books and listen to tapes every day to help me improve my business skills and knowledge. The reason I do that is it's sort of like exercising. If you stop exercising you will get weaker. If you stop reading books and/or listening to tapes, your skills will definitely deteriorate. So it is absolutely essential to be disciplined and read books or listen to tapes every day.

LL: I read one book per week. I recommend reading at least one to two chapters per day.

JL: Everyday.

DW: Use to a lot! Not much anymore. I don't have time now. I would recommend this kind of self-improvement study in the early days for everyone, however.

SW: Consistently. Your business will never grow larger than you do.

The most underrated activity in business is?

CE: Retailing, thinking you don't have to retail. If the product does not move, no one gets paid. People who say let everyone buy it wholesale don't understand that retail profit is the survival money for a new distributor the first 90 days they are in business. This is a business, so it's going to take some cash flow to operate it in the beginning. If anyone told you anything different, you should find that person and ask him or her why they lied to you.

JK: The most underrated activity in network marketing is self-development and goal-setting. Not nearly enough people do these two vital activities. Self-dependent separates the successes from the failures.

LL: Having a positive attitude at all times—how you think, so shall you be.

JL: Consistency.

DW: Building rapport with your customers, making them friends.

SW: Remaining value focused.

The most overrated activity in business is?

CE: Recruiting. It is not how many you recruit, it is how many you keep and how many you take down the leadership road to success. If you recruited 30 a month and in 90 days they all left, what good did it do you? There also are now 30 people somewhere telling 30 more people that your deal doesn't work. This is a warm-market business, and friends let friends know if they don't like something.

JK: The most overrated activity in network marketing is non-revenue-producing activities such as straightening one's office, making sure that the checkbook is properly set up, reading the manual for the 17th time. Now don't get me wrong—it is important to be organized and have an organized office. However, if you're not talking to people, you can'tsucceed in network marketing. Talk to some people, you will make some money. Talk to a lot of people, you will make a fortune.

LL: Research everything—don't overload yourself with too much info, just do it.

JL: Managing.

DW: Being the boss. Sometimes it is not so fun, like when dealing with negative people.

SW: Big money. "Hype is designed to recruit you, not educate you."

If you had to start your business all over again, what would you do differently?

CE: Nothing. I have had the privilege to work from day one with someone who I feel is the greatest mind in network marketing today, Dale Calvert. It has been an honor to have him as my mentor in this industry.

JK: If I had to start my business all over again, I would have spent a whole lot less time listening to the whiners and complainers. Thank God I don't have to do that anymore.

LL: Nothing. I think everything has its place. Every experience, good or bad, makes me who I am today and I'm thankful for them.

JL: I would focus initially on those people who bring usable skills to the table when they start.

DW: If I knew then, what I know now—a LOT—I would have gone online sooner, but now is still a good time to start if you have not.

SW: Spend less time on the wrong people.

What was your worst business decision?

CE: Letting people who I knew had the potential to do this business waste too much of my time. Spending too much time with the wrong people who we knew had great potential but never would get out of the rat race long enough to live their dreams. Bowling, softball, golf, etc. all got in the way of their dreams.

JK: My worst business decision ever by far was leaving the network marketing industry and getting a job. J-O-B stands for "jump out of bed" and "just over broke," and I definitely was very, very broke when I had my J-O-B.

LL: Not having the insight to buy Microsoft stock several years ago.

JL: Starting a business involving cars when I was 22. I have no interest in the area and had no experience or mentors. Consequently, I failed.

DW: Not going online sooner.

SW: Going to work for a corporation for sixteen and one half years. In other words, not realizing the truth behind network marketing sooner.

What was your best business decision?

CE: Joining New Image International.

JK: My best business decision was getting back into the network marketing industry. I have achieved financial independence and a lifestyle that very few people have today in the United States. Some people make a lot of money but they have no time. Some people don't make very much money but they have a lot of time on their hands. In network marketing we have both. It is truly a business of freedom.

LL: To help create Maxxis 2000, my current company, and also simultaneously to start network marketing. Those two decisions were the best for me to channel my energies into.

JL: Becoming self employed.

DW: Getting my own domain on the net!

SW: Taking the responsibility for my future instead of giving it to a boss.

What do you consider to be the main keys of your success?

CE: Faith, strong faith in God, other people, myself. I sincerely believe in people, I don't believe they are any big I's and little U's. The only difference between a big shot and a little shot is the big shot is a little shot that just kept on shooting. One of my favorite old movies is Boys Town. At the end of that movie he says there is no bad boys, only boys that need love and attention. I feel we could change that to people, not just boys. "I will persist and not be denied" should be everyone's motto. But the sad fact is 95% of the people hang up their dreams with their diplomas only to die at age 25 and not be buried until they are 65.

JK: The main keys to my success in network marketing are putting God first, self-development, having many wonderful leaders within my organization, and having an excellent company. These are all vital components, as far as being successful within the network marketing industry.

LL: Focus like a laser beam. Ability to see the big picture and knowing where I'm headed and why I'm going there. Persistence, enthusiasm, conviction, the ability to step out of the comfort zone because your comfort zone is your failure zone.

JL: Personal development and not giving up.

DW: Having a "Never-Give-Up" positive attitude and the World Wide Web.

SW: Value focus; People don't care how much you know until they know how much you care.

What's your success philosophy?

CE: God first, family second, business third. I want my family and friends to know that I did my best to serve with a servant's heart, that I inspired and lifted people up on a daily basis. I love what Mary Kaye Ash wrote in her book: "Treat everyone you meet as if they had an invisible sign around their neck saying 'MAKE ME FEEL IMPORTANT TODAY.'" The only thing that matters when we leave this world is what we did to make a difference in the lives of others. It won't matter where we lived, what kind of car we drove, or how big our bank account was.

JK: My success philosophy is simple: God first, family second, and business third.

LL: Follow your heart, listen to your inner voice (intuition). If you listen to that, every decision will be the best decision for you all the time.

JL: To make certain you're willing to pay the price, and if you are, learn everything and always be in an environment conducive to your goals.

DW: Treat folks like you want to be treated, but don't take any bull either! I'll bend, but I won't be walked on.

SW: Build people; people will build the business.

What about you has changed the most since finding success in business?

CE: One the best compliments I ever got from my husband was someone asked him had I changed since doing network marketing. His reply was, "Not at all, she has spent her life helping others and now she gets paid for it."

JK: Me! I had to step out of my comfort zone, I had to grow as a person, and that's so exciting to see in other people as they are building their business. It is really great that we are able to impact so many lives in network marketing in so many different ways.

LL: I now understand what it takes to become a leader and what the responsibilities are of being the center of strength for so many people. It has given me great joy and super happiness and a circle of friends and loved ones that encircle the globe.

JL: A clearer vision of why so many people never achieve their dreams.

DW: Probably my attitude toward money; it's not everything! Your creator, your family, they come first! If you are not happy without money, you won't be happy with it either. Fortunately, my wife Linda has been happy no matter how much we have had. I've learned a lot about life from her.

SW: Care for my fellow man.

What is the legacy you hope to leave?

CE: That I found favor with everyone I had any contact with, and I made a difference in the lives of the ones I love the most—my family and friends.

JK: The legacy I hope to leave is that I've made this a better world to live in and I definitely have a goal to help alleviate the terrible plight of starving children all over the world. There are tens of thousands of children starving to death every day, and that is totally unacceptable to me. So right now I am praying for a plan to help alleviate that, and some things are falling into place. It's very, very, very exciting to make a difference in the world.

LL: I want my great, great grandchildren to have my portrait over their fireplace and know that anything is possible if you want it bad enough.

JL: To carry on the success principles of those who came before me and hopefully empower as many people as possible to reach their full potential.

DW: Just for folks to say: "He was an honest, decent, hard-working man who cared about folks." More importantly, that the creator remembers me!!!

SW: To have touched as many people in a life-changing way. To have had a small but very significant piece of the positive influence in other lives.

Colleen Abbott

Age: 58

Family: Stanley E. Abbott, M.D. (husband); Children: Shire, Vaughan, Patrice, Lori, Michele, Christy, Michael, Ann, and Jenny; 18 grandchildren; and six great grandchildren

Employees: None

Year Started Business: 1996

Type Of Business: Alternative health business

Best Month (Gross Revenue): $15,000

Hours Worked Per Week During Start-Up: 60+ hours per week for over two years

Hours Worked Per Week Now: 20-35

Favorite Business Magazines: Forbes, Time, Newsweek

Favorite Business Books/Authors: First Things First—Stephen Covey, Being The Best You Can Be—John Kalench, Inside Network Marketing—Len Clements

Best Thing About Being Self-Employed: "I like being my own boss. No personnel reviews, no time clocks to punch in, no silly badge to wear, and no calendar controlling my life. I can work in comfortable clothes and shoes, take a break whenever I want, for as long as I want. I can work days or nights, weekends or weekdays, or not work if I choose to and go see my grandkids instead. My office space is truly mine; no superior or underling enters my home office to cause me extra work or worry. Also, I control the light, heat, and ambiance. I set my own goals and nobody says they are too high or unrealistic. I can create materials, advertising, flyers, and give them a personal touch, enjoying the creative process without harassment or deadlines. To say I'm having a ball would just about summarize the fun of doing my own thing."

Relaxes By: "So many good ways to relax, I'll just make a fun list. Bubble baths are underrated. Playing the piano is good for my soul. Reading a good book carries me away to a different place or exposes me to great ideas. Walking outside during any season of the year and seeing the mountains, watching the cloud formations, and listening to the sounds of birds always relaxes my body and mind. Being with someone I love is relaxing. Yoga and meditation always calms my soul. It is fun to watch a ball game. I don't get carried away, I just love to watch great athletes make difficult maneuvers seem easy. And often I look at photographs of nature or of loved ones. I have a little pond and waterfall I love to be next to. Life is good. Relaxing on the beach of Tahiti was incredible!"

Keeps in Shape Physically By: "I was recently in a minor car accident which acted as a reminder to take better care of my body, so I am paying more attention to the quality of foods I eat. I'm eating more fresh foods, whole grains, and easing off on the red meats. I don't smoke or use caffeine foods, so that part is good. Have a weight machine in the garage that I use two times a week to rebuild some of the injured muscles from the car accident. I go walking for 30 minutes each day for all-around good health. I have a Chinese friend who teaches me special exercises for body and mind, which also help my physical health."

Heroes: Dale Calvert—"He taught me that personal development was the key to success in life and everything you do. He is my mentor. One of Dale's favorite quotes is, 'People don't care how much you know until they know how much you care.' Another one is 'Ignorance is to continue to do what you have always done expecting different results. If nothing changes nothing changes.'" John Maxwell—"He's one of the best authors on leadership. His books have inspired me to become a better leader." Jim Rohn—"I love his tapes because 90% of his works are taken from the laws of sowing and reaping in the Bible. If you reap you must sow and I love his Challenge: 'Let others lead small lives but not you. Let others leave their future in someone else's hands but not you.'"

Admired Companies: Franklin-Covey, Inc., Morinda, Inc., Direct Sources.

Special Accomplishments: Member of Morinda's U.S. Founder's Club; holds the rank of Diamond Pearl; a recipient of the Black Pearl Global Bonus each quarter; in the top 50 global volume producers in 1999; in the top ten global "Top Performer" bonus earners in 1999; earned a free week vacation to Tahiti in 1999; won regional Toastmaster's speaking contests

Contact Colleen At: (801) 492-0790

Larry Edwards

Age: 51

Family: Monica (wife), 50; Sons Tad, 20, and Ryan, 15

Highest Education: Bachelor's of building construction from the Universitey of Washington

Year Started Business: May 1999

Type Of Business: Internet Website education

Market: Anyone with a computer and an Internet connection

Number Of Employees: "My wife and I work the business together, no other employees."

Best Month (Gross Revenues): $174,000

Hours Worked Per Week During Start-Up: 10 hours

Hours Worked Per Week Now: 30 hours

Favorite Business Magazines: Robb Report, National Geographic

Favorite Business Books And Authors: The Science of Getting Rich—Wallace D. Wattles, Jonathan Livingston Seagull—Richard Bach, Winning—Randy Ward

Relaxes By: Going to his summer home on a large mountain lake

Keeps In Shape By: Using Nordic Track five times a week.

Favorite Part Of Business: "Seeing the success of people who have come into the program after me."

Least Favorite Part Of Business: "Repetitive nature of sharing my story over and over."

Companies Admired: Microsoft, Cisco, Lucent Technologies

Heroes: "I have a problem with heroes, generally speaking. I once put a man on a pedestal; he could not live up to my expectations."

Special Accomplishments: Elected president of a national trade association at the age of 30. Larry was also honored at an MLM convention as the "Eighth Highest Income Earner in the World."

Favorite Quotes: I feel a lot MORE like I do right NOW than when I first got HERE.

Never be afraid to try something new. Remember, amateurs built the Ark, professionals built the Titanic.

Contact Larry At: (425) 317-8229

John Lloyd

Age: 55

Family: Single

Highest Education: Bachelor's in English and philosophy, Master's in communications

Year Started In Business: Started in network marketing in 1985; started present company three years ago

Type Of Business: Longevity nutrition, state-of-the-art anti-aging nutritional supplements

Market: Anyone with a heartbeat; greatest market: Baby Boomers.

Number Of Employees: One

Best Month (Gross Revenues): $25,000

Hours Worked Per Week During Start-Up: 60+

Hours Worked Per Week Now: "Very hard to say because I really don't 'work.' Is playing golf with my distributors work? My life is the 'work.'"

Best Thing About Being Self-Employed: "Doing what I want, when I want, with whom I want to do it, with money being of little to no concern; being able to shop without having to look at the price tag first; flying first class; giving a great deal to help the causes I believe in."

Favorite Business Books And Authors: Any and everything by Deepak

Chopra, especially Ageless Body, Timeless Mind; anything by Brian Tracy, especially the Psychology of Achievement (tape series); anything by Jim Rohn, especially The Art of Exceptional Living (tape series); and, of course, the Bible

Relaxes By: Reading, listening to music, meditating

Keeps In Shape By: Hiking Squaw Peak daily (elevation 2,608 ft., vertical climb 1,200 ft., 1.2 miles one way).

Favorite Part Of Job: The freedom it affords—getting to work with the most amazing people in the world and having an international business that the sun never sets on

Least Favorite Part Of Job: Having to some times wake up early to catch flights. "I normally wake up when I am done sleeping, I do not have an alarm on my clock."

The Person Who Most Influenced His Life: A high school teacher in Ed's junior year challenged him to step out of his comfort zone and be all that he could be. He went from a C- grade average to honor roll in six months and never looked back

Companies Admired: Amway—"They paved the path we now all walk."

Contact John At: (602) 494-4882

Michael Rideout

Age: 46

Family: One half-brother, three half-sisters, and his foster mom, all of whom live in Canada

Highest Education: Some college, majored in chemistry

Year Started Business: Started in network marketing in 1994; started with present company, Life Force International, in 1998

Type Of Business: Nutritional network marketing

Market: Everyone who desires to stay healthy, have more energy, and increase their income

Number Of Employees: None

Best Month (Gross Revenues): $32,000

Hours Worked Per Week During Start-Up: Approximately 30 to 40 hours the first three weeks. "I contacted everyone I could think of who I knew had an interest in an opportunity like this. I simply asked them to look up the Website or pull a fax-on-demand."

Hours Worked Per Week Now: Approximately 20 hours. "I work five hours four days a week, except when people come to visit the company, which is once a month. Then it is a matter of being a good host while they are in town. Some days the support calls are busier than others, and I like to schedule and balance my time between work and play."

Best Thing About Being Self-Employed: Awareness. "I am in charge of my own life. To be self-employed strengthens one's belief in self and improves your ability to make decisions faster. Also, the lifestyle difference is one of freedom that is not afforded to any other career—to be able to do what you want when you desire."

Favorite Business Magazines: Network Lifestyles, Millionaire, and Money Magazine

Favorite Business Books And Authors: The Magic of Thinking Big, How to be Happy Though Rich, and The Art of Happiness. These books have taught him more about relating to people, and that truly is the secret to reaching success in a business such as network marketing

Relaxes By: Ice skating, reading, exercising, listening to music, walking on the beach, chatting with friends, playing pool, dancing, sitting in the hot-tub with friends

Keeps In Shape Physically By: Works with a trainer. "I am really enjoying putting a lifestyle together that includes skating, biking, and working out in the gym."

Favorite Part Of Job: "I enjoy public speaking along with writing and creating any training materials that will help others succeed."

Least Favorite Part Of Job: Not being able to be in 10 different cities at once helping people

Favorite Quotes: As our case is new, we must think and act anew.—Abraham Lincoln, Nothing in life is to be feared, it is only to be understood.—Marie Curie; Have trust. Be a giver. Expect good. Be trustworthy.—Dayle Maloney

Contact Michael at: (800) 455-0096 or (858) 453-8394

Rich Strayer

Age: 63

Family: Evie (wife), his high school sweetheart; three daughters; five grand-sons; one granddaughter

Highest Education: Master's in electronic engineering from the University of Nebraska—Lincoln

Year Started Business: 1989

Type Of Business: Network marketing

Market: People who are committed to changing their health and financial future

Number Of Employees: None

Best Month (Gross Revenues): $13,000

Hours Worked Per Week During Start-Up: 50

Hours Worked Per Week Now: 45

Favorite Business Magazines: Home Office Computing, Success, and Home Business Magazine

Favorite Authors: Jim Rohn, Richard Poe, Michael Gerber

Relaxes By: Reading, walking, attending grandchildren's school activities

Keeps In Shape Physically By: Walking three miles a day; rebounding (mini-trampoline) for 15 minutes a day

Favorite Part Of Business: Visiting with downline members who are serious about building their business

Least Favorite Part Of Job: Fixing his computers when they are down

Companies Admired: Life Force International, Microsoft, Intel

Heroes: Teddy Roosevelt because he overcame childhood disease to become a leader

Special Accomplishments: Awarded USAF Commendation Medal for outstanding engineering management when in the U.S. Air Force

Best Thing About Being Self-Employed: "I can take the time to do things with my wife, adult children, and grandchildren when I want to."

Favorite Quotes: Always remember you are down on things you are not up on; Don't expect what you don't inspect; and What goes around comes around.

Contact Rich at: (303) 233-4152

Ed Wiens

Age: 48

Family: Ginger (wife); Children: Julie, 27; David, 24; Debbie, 22; Matthew, 14; Grandchildren: Jocelyn, 1; Maxwell, 9 months

Highest Education: College graduate

Number Of Employees: None

Year Started Business: 1993

Type Of Business: Independent Distributor for Nikken, Inc.

Best Month (Gross Revenues): $36,500

Hours Worked Per Week During Start-Up: "When we started our Nikken business, I was already working 50-60 hours per week, was President of a large Kiwanis Club, a school board member, volunteer fire department chaplain and served on several other community boards and committees. To get our Nikken business off the ground, I adopted a 'Whatever It Takes!' mindset. I had to fit it in and around what I was already committed to, none of which I could immediately phase out of. I have no idea how many hours I put in—a lot, as many as I could, whatever it took! Network marketing is the perfect opportunity for an already busy person to pursue. You can do it part time or full time, but you can't do it sometime. My philosophy is give it all you've got with whatever time you've got."

Hours Worked Per Week Now: "Our business is such an integral part of our personal and family life that I really don't know how many hours per week I put in. All I know is that my time is more my own now than it has ever been. I take plenty of time off and have periods of more intense activity than at other times."

Best Thing About Being Self-Employed: "Personal freedom is the sweetest thing about the kind of self-employment we have found. That is, after all, the objective of most who pursue self-employment. However, many who own their own business find that, in reality, their business owns them. That is not personal freedom. I love the fact that I can make life choices with Ginger and the kids that aren't guided entirely by lack of time availability or financial restriction."

Relaxes By: Fishing, playing golf, riding my Harley, spending a quiet evening or catching a movie with Ginger, playing games with the kids, going to a baseball game

Keeps In Shape Physically By: "Physical exercise is a needed area of focus for me. I've always joked that when I got rich, I was going to hire someone to exercise for me. Now that I could afford to do so, I realize it's still a challenge to maintain discipline in that area of life. Check back with me in a few months."

Favorite Part Of Business: Seeing people's lives changed physically, helping people see and grasp the opportunity to improve their life and actually fulfill their dreams, inspiring people to greatness, restoring their vision, and facilitating their pursuit of personal freedom

Least Favorite Part Of Business: Dealing with closed-minded skepticism that causes people to figuratively starve to death while surrounded by a banquet of opportunity that they are either oblivious to or choose not to see. Watching people give up on themselves or their dreams

Admired Companies: Nikken, Federal Express, and many of the old, pioneer network marketing companies that blazed the trail for what is now a thriving global industry

People Who Most Influenced Your Life: "My parents taught me the value of unwavering dedication to your mission in life. My dad taught me to believe in your beliefs, though questioned by others. My spirit of adventure into uncharted territory I learned from my mother, especially, who modeled the courage, faith, and vision necessary to forge ahead to new heights of accomplishment. My long time friend Joe Ellis helped me overcome by initial bias and discover the real truth about network marketing. He introduced me to many sources of personal growth and has continually challenged me to excellence."

Special Accomplishments: Achieved the Diamond level, member of the Presidents Club

Favorite Quotes: Task without vision is drudgery; vision without task is deception.—unknown; Good things come to those who wait, but only what's left over from those who hustle.—Abraham Lincoln; Never doubt your beliefs, never believe your doubts.—unknown; Everybody is ignorant, just on different subjects.—Will Rogers

Contact Ed At: (208) 455-2700

The Interviews

Colleen Abbott
(CA)

Larry Edwards
(LE)

John Lloyd
(JL)

Michael Rideout
(MR)

Rich Strayer
(RS)

Ed Wiens
(EW)

GETTING STARTED:

I'm starting a home business next month. I have a maximum of $3,000 in start-up capital. Where should I invest it?

CA: First thing I'd recommend is to park your $3,000 in a high-yield money market account, even if it is only for a short period, so your money is always working for you. Depending on the nature/market target of your home business, I would consult with a knowledgeable financial planner or other expert who knows your market/opportunity and can guide you to create short- and long-range business plans for the coming year. Decide on the tools you will need (computer, phone, fax, etc) and the best way to purchase/lease them to gain maximum tax advantage and preserve your capital. Skip purchases that reflect personal vanity. Unless you're on video on the net, the quality of your office furniture should not be a concern at this point. You need sturdiness and ease of function when you decide on desk, chair, filing cabinets, etc. Can't sell from an empty wagon so with your financial planner, determine inventory/product/office supplies and the best way (again, taxes are your biggest expense so work with your advisor to determine your good tax health with every business purchase) to obtain same. Shop/compare before you sign up for phone services, Internet, or leased equipment. Establish a record-keeping system and maintain it from day one. I wouldn't spend a penny until I had good answers to all the above issues. Avoid expensive advertising, including direct mail, until you know that such expenditures will add to your coffers, not drain them. Talk to people who have been successful in doing what you are about to do. Literally drain their brains because they are experts to learn from. Books are nice but hands-on experience is better. Learn what "price" they paid to become successful and re-evaluate whether or not you are willing to pay the same price. Take a realistic view of the marketplace. Are you going to stand out or is the field already too congested for you to succeed? Have you evaluated all the home-business options or have you fallen in love with the first pretty-faced business that came your way? Be wary of too much vanity, realize you are a beginner, and be well prepared before you start your business next month. Lastly, good luck and hope you realize your dreams.

LE: Invest it in the phone. Get a dedicated business line with three-way calling and call waiting. Get a fax on a dedicated line.

JL: Invest in the basics—a computer with a fax, two phone lines, and headset for the phone. Take a look at your environment. What will it take to make this work? Put your money there. Be VERY organized, then spend the rest for the basics, especially if you're in network marketing. For example, in my company's case, basics include cassette tapes; $3,000 is a minimum investment for a home business, IF you are really serious.

MR: Spend $400 to purchase the product, $400 to fly down to the company, $100 for the hotel room. See the company for yourself. This will strengthen your belief. People will believe you because you have been there and because they can hear it in your voice that it is real for you. Spend $200 to contact 30 people per month with a sample and information, $200 to invest in at least four books and two audio programs recommended by the team, and $400 for testing your advertising. Ask team leaders for advice on ads. With the remaining $1,300.00, reserve it for repeat advertising and sampling for the next three to four months. The best investment advice is not to buy a new desk, chair, filing cabinet, or fancy briefcase or rent an office until you are making a profit of more than $1,000.00 a month. Remember, fortunes have been made from kitchen tables.

RS: If you don't have a computer, buy one. Get on your company's autoship program, purchase online marketing tools that will make you more effective, join a lead-generation service, and keep the balance in reserve so you have staying power.

EW: Buy some product for personal and family use as well as demo and business-building purposes. Get some prospecting tools and some personal-growth materials. Get some basic business items (i.e. business cards), enhance your phone service (call waiting, three-way calling, perhaps a second phone line), and get some training specific to your company, products, and your industry.

I've just started a home business. My spouse has given me a six months to make it work. Any advice?

LE: Get to work FAST. Networking is a people business. Write out a list of the people you plan on contacting right away. If that list is less than 100 people, then get a day job.

JL: You have to make no less than a two-year commitment.

MR: First and foremost, sit down with your spouse and discuss what you both want from this extra venture. Whatever it is, better health, extra income, eventual time freedom, retirement income, there are certain things that must take priority for these six months to make any of your dreams come true. Discuss if six months is long enough. Would you open a restaurant or any other store and give it six months? Is six months a strong indicator of what your future will be? Would your spouse agree that they believe in you? Do you believe in yourself? Respect and honor each other by setting up parameters you both can agree to. Maybe date night is only twice a month instead of every week. Maybe the TV has to be turned off more to be able to focus on your ultimate goals. If you typically work an eight-hour day, are you willing to spend that sixth day of the week strictly working your business? If you added an hour a day to your efforts, do you think you would benefit faster? What is it you both desire? Be a team. After all, you are already a team, and when you help each other out, you both feel good. Get the family involved. Get the kids to put stamps on post cards. How about if your spouse would put a flyer on your church's bulletin board or hang up flyers for you at grocery stores? Do you think you would get someone to notice your opportunity more if your family believed in you and your opportunity and told a few more people? You bet you would. If you took one day a week and told your family that this day is fun day and all you did all day long was be with your family, would they appreciate you for this by honoring all the other days you are working extra hard because you want a better life for them? Communication is the key in this area. In my case, six months was enough for me to earn over $5,000.00 in this, my fourth attempt, in this industry. What you do determines your outcome. So do it fast, but be prepared to go long. If it is not working, ask for help and be teachable. When you take action, it makes all the difference. I would charge ahead full speed to create the biggest 90-day story I could and then do it again. Work with people who like and trust you. Visit your company ASAP. Build your belief and the rest is "EASY." Dayle Maloney said "I could have quit $7 million ago." For me, I often realize I could have quit before the $20,000 checks came in. I am very glad I didn't. Of the businesses that fail in this industry, it is often due to lack of commitment and many times that is a lack of capital committed to the growth. Once you make an investment you will work harder—that is just human nature. You have a vested interest. You will need tools, such as a good desk, bookcase, file cabinet, etc. I just set up a little office, and I spent $1,000.00 for supplies and $1,000.00 for equipment. Most likely you will need a fax, phone, scanner, and maybe a computer. Remember, I now have the cash flow to set up an office. I was in network marketing for four years before I purchased my laptop computer. The money you need is best spent to introduce people to products and to promote the company. Little, if any, money should be spent on equipment in your start-up phase. All the computers, beautiful furniture, nice office, or framed artwork will not make you a dime if you are not contacting people and sampling your companies products.

RS: Take massive action every waking moment using a proven system but also take time to spend with the spouse.

EW: Consult with those already in your business who have built it quickly and know how to teach others how to do it. Learn and implement immediately. Make sure your communication with your spouse is thorough about what this opportunity means to you and your desire to provide for his/her long-term well-being. Have him/her visit with other spouses of successful players in your business. Treat your new opportunity seriously right away, as an assignment that you must complete successfully, with no other alternative. They say it takes money to make money.

Should I try to get a small business loan for my start-up capital or just try to get by with my own limited finances?

CA: Know your actual or projected financial needs down to the last dollar. Whether you are getting by on a shoestring budget or getting a small-business loan, you need a road map to get you where you are going. Think of the intricate planning necessary to blast off a rocket and the cost overruns that happen without specific parameters every step of the way. Cost control and planning go hand in hand. This road map will clearly indicate whether you must have a chunk of capital at the beginning or can get by with limited finances. Why go into debt and get a loan if you don't need one? Why avoid getting the necessary loan when it will enable you to get over the starting hump and create some momentum in your new business? Don't guess. Evaluate the facts and get the finances according to the facts, not hunches. It takes discipline to have a successful home business. Remember, you are the only boss, and the buck stops with you.

JL: It's all according to the extent of what is needed. In my company's case, getting a loan was not needed. Also, it is very difficult to secure such a loan. I say go it alone. Reach for the ceiling, but go for the stars.

LE: Networking is a people business. It takes people, not money, to make money in this business. I would not put myself into debt with this business.

MR: Get by with your own capital. Do not get a loan.

RS: Have a garage sale and self-fund your activities. That is why I love the Internet, there are a lot of free resources available to build a network-marketing business online.

EW: Most businesses are not started with cash on hand. Instead, some form of other people's money (credit, business, or personal loan, etc.) is leveraged to get off the ground. Realize the difference between consumer debt and investment debt. If you finance your start-up with a loan or credit, as most do, just work it like a business, not a hobby.

Do you consider yourself an "early adopter" of new technology?
CA: No, I was intimidated by the computer for many years. I'm probably a moderate when it comes to speed of adopting new technology. Now I own two computers, etc., and wonder how I ever got along without using them. E-mail is fast and free. Once I catch on to a techno tool, I learn to love it.
LE: I have resisted technology like the plague. A strange thing to say for someone who is making a living off of the Internet. My biggest fear is that it's too easy to hide behind the technology and get away from the people.
JL: Late bloomer in computer usage; early on in everything else.
MR: Yes.
RS: Yes.
EW: Yes.

If you use a toll-free phone number, what is your primary use for it?
CA: Well, my kids are always willing to call me on my nickel!!! For business purposes, I put it on the name sticker that accompanies everything that leaves my office (mail, samples, tapes, CDs, literature). It is printed on my business card and on any advertising I do. I always give it to a new prospect or partner and encourage them to stay in touch with me as their working partner. So the primary use is to facilitate open communication between prospects, partners, and myself.
JL: I mail thousands of tapes weekly and run ads in major publications. A toll-free number is a must.
MR: Ad responses and voice-mail communication within my organization.
RS: For checking my messages when I am traveling.
EW: I currently have one that I use selectively for prospects or some personally sponsored distributors outside of my immediate area.

How do you use voice mail?
CA: Voice mail sets a tone of openness to encourage people to leave me a message if they happen to call when I'm out or on the other line. Some folks don't like to leave a message, so I look up their number on the Caller ID and give them a call. For those who do leave a message, I try to respond to within 24 hours.

Describe your computer system and how you use computers in your business.
CA: Microsoft Windows 98 and Microsoft Office on a Pentium II 400 MHz computer with a 6.4 GB hard drive, and a CD-ROM. I also have a Xerox color printer, a laser printer, and a Xerox office copier/printer with software for large print jobs. Word processing can make any business look professional. Printing on company letterhead is a good idea. Keeping a financial record on the computer is a great idea. Making creative flyers and presentations is fun and makes you look polished. I also use CDs from my company for instant computer presentations about my home-business opportunity. The computer links me to the world via the Web, where I spend a good part of each business day communicating with my global partners via e-mail or linking to company other related business sites for the latest information about my business. I can access the activities of my entire downline on a daily basis via the net. And it is fun to create greeting cards and play games on the computer. What a tool! We have two computers in our family, both connected to the Web.
LE: I have a Macintosh computer, printer, and scanner. I am on the Internet a few hours a day. E-mail is a huge communication tool for me.
MR: A Pentium-based computer with Windows 98, a scanner, a Zip drive, and a laser

Technology Utilized

	Fax*	Fax-on-Demand	Toll-Free	Voice Mail	Computer	Email	Internet	Website	Email Auto-Responders
Colleen Abbott	✓	✓	✓	✓	✓	✓	✓	✓	
Larry Edwards	✓				✓	✓	✓	✓	✓
John Lloyd	✓	✓	✓	✓	✓	✓	✓	✓	✓
Michael Rideout	✓	✓	✓	✓	✓	✓	✓	✓	✓
Rich Strayer	✓	✓	✓	✓	✓	✓	✓	✓	✓
Ed Wiens	✓	✓	✓	✓	✓	✓	✓	✓	✓

* Dedicated fax line

printer.

RS: Two Pentium II computers running Windows 98, as well as a couple of printers.

EW: For my first 18 month, I had no computer and still had tremendous growth. Just five years later, this is a different time, however. I am currently upgrading my five-year-old PC to a new Pentium III, 700 MHz system. I am also acquiring my first laptop, a Pentium II, 400 MHz notebook. I also use a scanner, a color printer, and a laser printer/fax.

What software do you consider in the "must-have" category?

CA: I prefer Corel WordPerfect, but maybe that's because my son-in-law wrote the program. It is easy to use.

LE: Basic stuff, such as a word-processing program.

JL: Any good spreadsheet program. The same goes for word processing, photographs, scanning, faxing, and graphics software. Keep it simple; don't overload.

MR: Act 2000, Quickbooks, Microsoft Word.

RS: World Merge, The Classified Connection, FFA Blaster, ListManager, Text Bomber, and ClipMate along with Microsoft Access.

EW: A good word processor, spreadsheet, and presentation program (Microsoft Office 97 has served me well.). Also important is a good contact management program. I use the PC-based Franklin Covey program.

What other technologies, if any, do you use in your business?

CA: My cell phone brings my office with me wherever I go. Just program call forwarding if expecting an important call. Sure beats hunting for a phone booth on the highway when I need to make a call.

LE: I try to avoid too many techno toys.

JL: A cell phone is a must.

MR: Cell phone and laptop computer.

RS: E-mail listserver to keep in touch with my downline, weekly training teleconference calls which are recorded for my people who can't get on the call.

EW: I have a portable cell phone that I go everywhere with, and one in each of the vehicles that I drive regularly. I have been a devoted Palm Pilot user for nearly three years. I keep my schedule and appointments, phone directory, and notes/memos on it. It also serves as somewhat of a journal I can recreate any single day of my life since I began using it.

Name up to five personal favorite business Websites our readers can benefit from:

CA: www.morinda.com, www.tropical-express.com, www.noni.com, and www.sixfigureincome.com.

LE: www.skynary.com/ednet and www.skynary.com/monica1/go.

MR: www.bestfares.com (save on travel) and www.lifeforce-intl.com.

RS: FreeLeads.com/team/cash4u and www.sixfigureincome.com.

EW: www.nikken.com, www.teamdiamond.com, www.upline.com , www.NMLifestyles.com, and www.jimrohn.com.

Of all the technology you use, rank your top three:

CA: My all-time favorite techno tool is to use the e-mail on the computer/Web. It is hard to make myself write a letter since e-mail is so fast and efficient. Second choice would still be the telephone with three-way calling, caller ID, and voice-mail package. A telephone call can turn the world around in a few seconds. When an e-mail isn't providing the personal touch, I grab the phone and speak in person. Last, but not least, when it isn't possible to send information via the net, I love using the fax machine. Somebody needs a form or an article right now, I just fax it and the deed is done. These three tools are the core of my home-business communication. There is one more tool I'd like to recommend the use of. It doesn't quite fit this techno category: That is U.S. Priority Mail and Global Mail. These services are fast and economical, plus they make you look good to the person on the other end. He/she feels important that he/she is receiving something other than ordinary mail from you.

LE: Phone, Computer, Internet.

JL: E-mail, Voice Mail, Cell Phone.

MR: Cell Phone, E-mail, Fax-on-Demand.

RS: Computer, Fax, Teleconference Calls.

EW: Cell Phone, Palm Pilot, Computer.

MARKETING & ADVERTISING:

Do you market on the Internet?

CA: No. Have tried it a few times, placing ads here and there. Have not found the right advertising combination yet. My Web address is on all literature, samples, etc., so that is a form of Internet marketing.

LE: I market an Internet program, but I do not use the Internet as a marketing tool.

JL: Yes, overall, which includes my distributors.

MR: I don't personally do a lot of Internet marketing. However, I have a large segment within my organization who do so very successfully. Some of my other groups do very well retailing product on the Internet, too.

RS: Yes, I promote the Web version of Six-Figure Income Magazine(www.sixfigureincome.com) using all the techniques I teach my downline.

EW: Yes, through my personal, company-approved Website that I have on my business cards and that I distribute to any leads. This is a new arena for me so I am still feeling my way along. It's too soon for me to know just how this venue will be fully utilized.

Approximately what % of your sales originate from this marketing?

JL: About 10%.

MR: 50%.

RS: 95%.

EW: Too soon to tell.

Do you use direct mail?

CA: Yes, but not with a lot of success. What works the best for me and my market is using the "warm market" approach of people who know people. I have experimented with direct mail several times as it sounds like a good idea, but my product/opportunity is so unique that the message needs to be delivered by a real human being, not a piece of paper. People usually have questions that go unanswered when they only have the motivation of words on a piece of paper. I have bought lists or put together lists and created flyers or post cards that were mailed. The response didn't justify the expense so I stopped.

LE: I believe in warm market, team building. In 35 weeks, I built a network of 85,000 people around the world by sponsoring 15 people I knew and using three-way calling to help them do the same. I recognize there are really only two things you can do in networking: 1.You can talk to people that you know. 2.You can talk to people that you do not know. I prefer #1. However, many people in my group are successful with the second style. I recommend people avoid the only other possible course of action: keep the business a secret and talk to nobody.

JL: Yes, I mail out hundreds of thousands of tapes.

MR: I used to do a lot of direct mail (postcards). However, at this time a very small percentage of my organization does direct mail.

RS: No.

EW: I haven't. Some of my group have and I've supplied info for them.

Approximately what % of your sales originate from this marketing?
JL: 40%.
MR: 5%.

Do you use print media (e.g. magazines, newspapers, card decks)?
CA: Yes, I have created 20 ads for newspapers and magazines. Have targeted specific markets with these various ads. What has worked the best for me was a little rhyme I created for the business opportunity market and it was the cheapest, too. In General, I spent too much money for too little business benefit. I'll admit it was fun to design the ads but not profitable in the end. Recently I placed an ad in a college alumnus magazine and got some great responses from it, but no new partners. So I am back to the "warm market" principle as it works the best for me.

JL: Yes. Display ads and classified ads in major publications.

MR: I currently am running five ads in local magazines and newspapers.

RS: Yes, I advertise my Website in local newspapers.

EW: I have to a small degree. I've participated in a couple of ad programs spearheaded by some of my distributors.

Approximately what percentage of your sales originate from this marketing?
CA: About 1%. I can do better talking to people in the Post Office line than I have done in advertising, so I have backed away from a big advertising budget.
JL: 20%.
MR: 5%.
RS: 2%.
EW: Very small.

Do you use radio and/or TV advertising?
CA: Yes, as my company airs a free, one-hour promotion program weekly on Dish Satellite Network on the 901 business channel. Often, I'll have prospects come to my home to view it. I make sure my downline in North America is taking advantage of the free advertising. Often I'll connect a new prospect with this airing who lives in another state and call after the program for a discussion.

JL: Yes, I have my own radio program. About 15% of my total sales come from the radio program.

MR: At the time of this writing I will be running a radio show and the results are yet to be determined.

RS: No.
EW: No.

What other kinds of marketing do you utilize?
CA: Often people will stop me in a parking lot when they see the magnetic signs on my Audi advertising this unique juice. I place information newspapers on counters (with the owner's permission) anywhere I am, in state or out of state. These information newspapers are professionally printed and have the experiences of my personal downline in them. Often people call me as a result of these newspapers. When I'm waiting for my car to be washed, I might leave a couple of entry forms for a free trip to Tahiti (a company monthly drawing), and later find people in the computer who have registered for the trip and bought product and became serious business partners. The best kind of marketing is to be healthy, happy, and listen to people. I always carry CDs, tapes, and printed marketing materials to give to the nice stranger I just met in line who is complaining about a health problem, not enough time, or not enough money. Depending on the circumstances I might give away a free sample. Even my Avon lady buys from me because I gave her a free sample of one of my related juice products! I write marketing letters to people who I want to educate about my business and give the financial footprint of my opportunity. Sometimes, a scientific study is my best marketing tool; other times a testimonial does the trick. I have brought people from overseas into the corporate office and research lab so they could see for themselves what a tremendous opportunity this home-based business is. Flexibility and moment determine my marketing approach; I believe a person should not rely on just one tool or type of marketing.
JL: The three-foot rule: no one comes within three feet of me who does not receive one of my tapes.
MR: I believe in three-way calls, conference calls and fly-ins. The fly-ins are so important because the people investigating the company have a personal experience, get to meet the owners and principles, see the actual production of the products and have the opportunity to have their questions answered face to face.
RS: Personal contact.
EW: I have supported some of my distributors with fair booths, mall shows, etc. I am currently working with some distributors in a new e-mail-based direct-mail program.

Do you recommend using a toll-free number in advertising? Why or why not?
CA: Yes. Give the reader a reason to call you and then make it easy for him/her to contact you. I also include my e-mail address, as some people like a little distance between you and them in their first inquiry. Make sure you have a good rate on the toll-free number or the person will sense your money anxiety during the phone call. The phone call can be short with the purpose of getting a name and address to send an information packet, etc.
LE: If you want to advertise nationally, yes, get a toll-free number with a short recorded message, so the caller can leave their name and number.
JL: Absolutely. It is expected in our society.
MR: I have used both an 800 number and a toll number. I definitely received more responses with the 800 number but not necessarily quality leads. I recommend using a toll number because you really want to sponsor people who have a prosperity consciousness and do not grumble about the little stuff like a long-distance call. Test the method, measure the results, and if you can afford it, try both with the same ad.
EW: Yes. It's proven that the easier you make it for people to respond, the more likely they will. If they do, the greater the likelihood they can become interested in what you

have to offer. Anymore, toll-free numbers are very inexpensive to have.

Where do you market?
CA: Personally, I work locally. But through my group I work everywhere. (However, I do have personally sponsored partners in several countries and I work directly with them.) This answer may sound confusing, but I have a consumable product that is accepted in many countries already, and I am eager to get into more markets. The actual process of marketing is indirect, as I develop a human network around the globe to do what I do locally, which is to tell people about this incredible juice and its attached financial opportunity.
LE: I market a worldwide business, I do three-way calls internationally.
JL: Locally, nationally, and internationally.
MR: I market locally and nationally.
RS: Internationally on the Internet.
EW: Anywhere and everywhere. I have found it's common for people to get so caught up, however, in pursuing the markets everywhere but in their own back yard (the "greener-grass" syndrome). Most of my best success has come from the three-foot rule. Talk to those whose paths you cross within the context of daily life. You never know where the word-of-mouth network will take you or your business. We have business in every state, Canada, and overseas just as a result of the long range ripple effect of one telling one person.

How should someone set up their home office to maximize its effectiveness?
CA: The suggestions I would give are to be physically and psychologically comfortable in whatever place selected. My office is on the main floor of my home, close to the front door, and by a bathroom reserved for my visitors. It has a window looking out on the front of the house where I can also see beautiful mountains. The room is small, has a closet for storage, books shelves, and a filing cabinet. On one wall I have a huge world map and pictures of many of my international partners. Someone else might want a white board to list current projects. Because I'm a visual person, I also post motivational sayings and pictures of my family to keep me company while I work. The computer and printer are near my files. The telephone sits on my desk, and I have a small work table for ongoing shipping projects. The fax machine sits on a small storage unit where I store current financial records. I have two chairs with good back support which swivel. One is my working chair and the other is a guest chair. I have comfort, light, privacy, and visual stimulation. My files and computer are handy and I have a project table. The fax doesn't take up extra space as it sits on top of a storage unit where I can easily use it.
LE: What I did was to take one extra bedroom in the home and turned it into an office library. I need one specific place to go to conduct my thoughts.
MR: If possible, designate a separate room for your office. Utilize at least two phones. One phone has to be only for business calls. Use an answering machine and be professional. You need to keep good records on your prospects. Make sure you have a phone

message book and an appointment book. You need to create a schedule and stick to it. This IS a business. When you are financially able, buy a fax machine and computer. Use a comfortable chair. A headset and speaker phones are very useful. I don't have a family now at my home, but at one time I tried to do my business with children around, and as soon as the ground rules were set, there weren't any problems.

RS: Separate from their living quarters. Plenty of room to spread out.

EW: Communication is a crucial part of the home-based business today, so don't skimp on communication technology. Get a phone line just for business, separate from the personal family number. I recommend a dedicated fax line and even a dedicated Internet hook-up (high speed, if available in your area). Try to set up a workspace that is out of the day-to-day flow of the household activities, a separate room, if possible. When getting started, however, don't worry about having the ideal home office setup. Just get started! Tom Peters, the business management guru, once wrote a book entitled Thriving on Chaos. Expect that to be somewhat descriptive of life with a growing, live in-home business. I've often joked about not having a filing system, but a piling system. If you're a neat freak and can still be productive, great. But the bottom line is get the business of the business done. Whatever it takes!

Are there any ground rules you've established for yourself, family, etc. for operating at home successfully?

CA: Since my children are all grown and my husband is a gentleman, I have it easy working at home. If things were different, I would post a schedule of my working time and non-working time on the outside door to my office and then close the door and stick to that schedule. It would be important to enjoy my family during non-working hours so my working time (closed door) wouldn't be resented or interrupted. Weekly family councils to coordinate family member's needs should allow for a discussion of time and activities. Sounds simple, but it must be a challenge for family members to adjust to the presence of a home business and respect it as a business.

LE: I have established no ground rules for my home-based business. I wanted the freedom and flexibility that a home-based business gives. Family first.

JL: I treat it like what it is—my business. And it is operated as such.

MR: There needs to be an understanding that TV and voices are kept at reasonable volume during conference calls, etc. There are times to work and schedules to be kept and communication is the key. Balance your fun and your business (even though this business is really fun). Set your limits and your expectations and keep on keeping on.

RS: No, my kids are gone and my wife leaves me alone to work.

EW: I've been blessed with a great family. With our business, everyone is on the team and knows how important the game is. The phone must always be answered courteously, especially important for teenagers in a day when most of them (guys anyway) answer with a "you're-interrupting-my-sleep" guttural grunt. Phone messages must always be completed (time/date/action required) and written legibly. When a special event is coming up or business guests are coming, everyone does their part to prepare. I don't have specific hours I keep in my in-home office, though I tend to be a night person, especially when at home. The key is be diligent and disciplined, yet flexible and spontaneous.

Do you consider working at home an advantage or disadvantage to your business overall?

CA: I love working at home and it is definitely an advantage for my type of business. It would be silly to rent an office space downtown, dress for the image of success everyday, commute to my office, and then do exactly what I need to do in the comfort of my own home, barefooted. The phone, fax, and e-mail allow me to do everything necessary to build and support a thriving home business, with tax write offs to boot.

LE: The advantage of having a business at home is not having to commute. However, I need to get into some structured outside activities, just to get out of the house.

JL: A 100% advantage. It is a day and night thing that allows total flexibility in every aspect. You just have to learn when to turn off the phones.

MR: I have worked somewhat at home most of my life, although not all my photography studios were at a home location. Now, it is quite easy for me to have the self-discipline to work at home, but I think many people allow the everyday disruptions to interfere with their work time. The choice is yours. Do yourself a favor and have a family meeting and establish what you need to happen.

RS: BIG advantage.

EW: The advantages far outweigh any disadvantages.

Do you farm out any of your work?

CA: Yes, I hire bookkeeping help and review the tax laws with my financial planner and **CPA,** who does my taxes. In my opinion, financial matters and bookkeeping could be farmed out. Mailing in bulk could be farmed out. A part-time secretary might be a good idea to handle correspondence. Kids could be hired to distribute flyers and other local advertising items.

LE: I run a one-man show. I like to wear all of the hats. I like the variety.

JL: All manual tasks—stuffing envelopes, mailing tapes, creating lists, everything that feels like a "J-O-B" (Jumping Out of Bed).

MR: Yes, graphic artwork and voice-mail service. I also plan to have an outside fulfillment center this year. I encourage people to consider their budget and their time schedule when deciding to farm out any activity. It will cost more money in immediate cash flow, but it may free up your limited and valuable time to associate with new and existing friends in a manner that is good for your life and will to expand your business.

RS: Yes, I farm out follow-up e-mail contact with new affiliates and members. Never farm out phone contact with downline and prospects, however!

EW: Yes, anything that I can pay someone else to do that keeps me freed up to do what I do best I do it. We retain the services of a bookkeeper and an accounting firm. I have professionals I look to for investment and legal advice. My daughter helps me regularly in the office fielding calls, filing, faxing, organizing, and performing general office work. My wife, Ginger, has someone who helps with the housework regularly, and we hire a lawn maintenance firm. Because our business is so relational with our distributors, some of the personal communication could never be farmed out. My distributors don't have to go through a maze of answering machines or paging services to reach me. I make myself easily available to them. I don't even consider it a terrible imposition when my cell phone rings while I'm on the golf course or out fishing—what a great place to be at work! Not every business is so portable or flexible. If I don't want to be reached, that's easy enough to arrange.

Do you encourage or discourage... Partnerships?
CA: I don't want a legal partner. That's why I'm an independent distributor by title. Another meaning of the question could be the formation of a legal corporation for tax purposes which can be a wise, tactical decision for a home-business owner.
LE: I discourage sharing a distributorship. I do encourage having a working, team-building relationship with the organization.
JL: Discourage. Like marriages, they can be dissolved.
MR: Legal partnerships need to be drawn up carefully with good counsel and your partner must have the same goals and expectations as you do. A partner can lighten the burden of building a business, but the wrong partner can become the burden. My mother used to say, "partnership is a leaky ship."
RS: Discourage.
EW: Typically, no. In network marketing, sponsors work as partners with their distributorships anyway. So why run the risk of future complications that can easily occur with a partnerships? In rare instances (family members, other extenuating circumstances), I will recommend it.

Do you encourage or discourage... hiring family members?
CA: I would discourage co-mingling of boss/employee relationships with family role relationships. The two sets of value systems/expectations are bound to cause confusion over time. You can't fire family members, but you may want to if they are poor employees for you.
LE: I like General Schwarzkopf's quote best: "It amazes me still that when the U.S. government sends me overseas to organize 100,000 men, my troops jump to my every command. However, when I come home and ask my sons to mow the lawn, all I get is, 'Geee-wizzz dad,' and a lame excuse."
JL: Never. Nepotism should be a criminal offense. It has darkened more good intentions than anything ever created and destroyed credibility.
MR: Depends on the family. That's a tough one. If they will live the business, yes. If it is just to hire them to help them out, then no. If it is the kids, then absolutely. They would benefit from the experience.
RS: Encourage.
EW: There are some advantages to hiring family members (tax-wise and otherwise). I love the values and culture of a family run business, where everyone takes ownership of a common cause, and works diligently for the benefit of all involved. I've been blessed with an extremely close, very supportive immediate family. Three of our children have their own distributorships and our youngest son is looking forward to being 18 so he can enroll; he already has fellow 8th graders who want to be on his team. The downside to actually hiring family members is that they may not treat their hired assignment quite as diligently as an outside job. Expectations have to be clearly delineated and accountability systems in place.

When legal issues arise, what's your usual response?
CA: I first want to know the problem and what circumstances make it a legal issue. Then I would want to know the exact law and determine why that law was broken (unintentionally or intentionally). I would examine the moral (spirit of the law) aspects of the problem to see if an informal settlement can be reached without resorting to attorneys and hearings. Even if I feel I'm in the right, I would make every effort to understand the remedy/problem from the other person's point of view. If the person is vindictive and wants his day in court, I would hire a good attorney and be well prepared to go to the

mat. But whenever possible, I would seek to restore good will and settle the matter out of court. My time, reputation, and personal energy are important and not to be wasted in revenge. But if I fight, I fight to win.

LE: "Is this a pyramid?" I love this question. I have more fun with it than almost anything else. Of course it is a pyramid, I would not be involved if it wasn't. The pyramid structure is the foundation of every major corporation in America. Can you name me one corporation that is not structured like a pyramid? How about the back of the U.S. dollar bill? I find that all legal questions stem from misunderstood rumors. I take them head on, and have a little fun with them.

JL: None. I never had any. I do not attract negative energy.

MR: I let my lawyers handle it. I give it no energy unless it can be resolved easily.

RS: I call my Pre-Paid Legal Attorney.

EW: I've always held to the principle that communication is the key to understanding. Legal issues usually arise due to a breakdown of communication. Ideally, a clear atmosphere of communication could avert a legal battle. Depending on the issue and what's at stake, I would rather walk away from a conflict appearing to have lost than to spend the time, money, or energy on a fight just to prove a point. I was taught long ago to never get in a fight with a chimney sweep—even if you win, you still come away dirty. However, if the consequences are serious enough, I'll fight with no intention of losing.

Does earning a lot of money improve the quality of your life, and if so, in what ways?
CA: Yes, earning a lot of money does improve the quality of my life, as it gives me a handle on the future. I can enjoy today and put aside for tomorrow and help those in need without walking by because I have no extra funds to help. It is a joy to sit by my fire with myhusband and not worry about having enough money since he is now retired. Most people retire to fear. One serious medical problem and many retired people lose what little life savings they have. We can travel when we choose (and traveling takes serious money), replace cars instead of hanging on to them and hoping they won't break down, and not shudder when the cashier rings up the total at the grocery store. Perhaps the greatest blessing extra income brings is the ability to help others, including our children, when there is a need. Our children won't have to shoulder any financial responsibility for us as we get older. There is a lot of dignity in being comfortable and having plenty to share with others. Once I heard a marketer say he wanted to earn a lot of money so he could write a large tithing check every month. I like that attitude.

LE: It has always been about choices for me. I can make more choices if I have more money.

JL: Of course it does. Lack of money is the root of all evil. Money may not be everything, but it ranks right up there with oxygen. Money is God in action. Money is positive energy. Energy is positive love. Study all crimes; 80% of them are related to money. God created us to be abundant, not "lacking." We do not serve God by lack and limitation. Lack of money leads to stress and stress is the greatest free radical damager on the planet. Free radical damage is the cause of ALL aging and disease. It is the stress factor that inspires me to make a great deal of money. AND I am here to help heal the planet and help children in many ways. Money helps me do this and this is my mission.

MR: Well like Sinatra said, "I've been rich and I've been poor. Rich is better." I can say the same. I like to make things happen and money helps to do that. Having a lot of money only helps your life if you have your values and principles straight before you have the money.

RS: Yes, you have a different attitude about life.

EW: Coming from a ministry background, I've been around the mountain a few times when it comes to the matter of money, wealth, materialism, etc. In short, money is neither good or bad. It is only a tool. In the hands of good people, it does good things. In the hands of evildoers, it wreaks destruction. In our 21st century world, it is a tool that wields unprecedented power and influence. I've also concluded this: Money in abundance doesn't change you, it only makes you more of what you already are. Obviously, money can't buy happiness, but neither does poverty. I've personally worked with the poor for years (in inner-city social programs), and I can tell you the poor can't help the poor. It takes monetary resources passing through the hands of good people to feed, clothe, and care for the needy. Does having more money ensure you of improvement in your quality of life? Absolutely not. Can it improve your quality of life? Absolutely. Financial abundance can provide comforts of life, enhance your lifestyle, enable you to give to causes you believe in and care about and help you show your love to your friends and family. It's done all of that for us and for others through our efforts, which is another reward in itself. Kathleen Deoul, Nikken's 1999 Distributor of the Year says it so eloquently: "I never apologize for the money I make in this business, because every single dime earned represents someone whose life I've touched and maybe even saved." What a way to make a living! Zig Ziglar said it best: "Money isn't everything, but it ranks right up there with oxygen! You have to have some just to survive." Several authors have helped me tremendously when wrestling with my own perspective (and latent guilt) about monetary gain. Among them are: Peter Daniels (How to be Happy Though Rich) Paul Zane Pilzer (God Wants You to be Rich) Kevin Gerald (Pardon Me, I'm Prospering).

Best general tax advice?

CA: Pay what you owe and pay it in time. Don't pay one penny more than you owe, which means you understand the laws and regulations concerning home businesses and claim the proper deductions. Keep a precise paper trail in case of an audit. Form a corporation that fits your business and helps lower your tax liability. Plug every tax leak possible by seeking professional advice.

LE: Get yourself a professional tax consultant, not necessarily a tax accountant.

JL: Pay them! Keep detailed records, never discard a receipt, always write who was present on entertainment receipts, make sure your day planner reflects same, have a good accountant, and form a trust!

MR: Remember to put away money every month. Keep good records. Learn to use programs like Quicken or Quickbooks. Hire a good CPA. Unless you are an accountant type, a lot of effort is needed to keep the books, and farming this work out would free up time for you. Take a simple tax course.

RS: Make your monthly IRS and state tax deposits.

EW: Get some advice. There are many strategies for the self-employed person to follow in order to keep more of what you make. Do your homework, find the plan and people that you're comfortable with. Stay ahead of the daily disciplines required when your numbers are small and you'll reduce your risk of problems when the numbers grow.

Best general investment advice?

CA: Always have your money working as an asset for you, night and day. Don't tie up your money in liabilities. Think of money as an active work horse, not a sleepy donkey tied up in expensive toys and houses where it does not work for you. Avoid credit card debt. Have multiple steams of income, not just one source of income. Keep learning about the use of money to duplicate itself. Don't be passive about your money.

LE: I made myself debt free as soon as possible. Best investment decision I ever made.

JL: Buy low, sell high! If your NETWORK MARKETING is public, which is the ideal case, invest in that stock. Always use pros to invest and pay yourself first a minimum of 10 to 15%.

MR: Invest in something you enjoy and want to learn more about. Never invest more than you can afford to lose. Keep greed out of your investment equation. Seek good advice and verify from several people the quality and stability of the investment.

RS: Invest in yourself, in equipment that can help you leverage yourself, and in maintenance of your physical property. Then invest what is left over with the help of a financial planner.

EW: Find good mentors and learn from them. Get comfortable with a general investment mindset that suits your personality and aggressive or conservative game plan. Don't wait until you have huge amounts to invest before you start a systematic investment program. Small, consistent steps can grow significantly over time. Technology has made this a new day when it comes to individuals taking charge of their own investments programs. Read, attend a seminar, learn, and implement.

You're in business already, and you've just received a windfall of $20,000. What would you do with it?

CA: Go back to your master business plan and see if an infusion of all or part of the $20,000 would help your business surge forward. If you have had to pinch so hard to get your business up and running that you have denied your spouse/family financially, take some of that money and insert it into your family life where it will make a real difference. Tithe the windfall and the rest will stretch to exceed what you gave away because you won't have a greedy heart. Is there a life insurance policy that got canceled to save funds? If so, put it back in place as part of your sound financial management. Invest in stocks or annuities (according to market conditions). Live within your budget and let this extra money act as a financial umbrella and avoid the temptation to nickel and dime away this small fortune.

LE: Invest it with my broker and let it grow to $40,000. Then spend the $20,000.

JL: Put it right back into my business. NEVER SPEND IT. Give at least 10% - 15% to church or charity. Always GIVE.

MR: Take a trip for a month and write a book. The trip will clear your mind and rejuvenate your spirit to pursue the next part of your journey.

RS: Invest it.

EW: Eliminate high interest debt (credit cards, etc.), make a needed capital purchase (equipment, etc.), invest a portion of it.

What do you lead with: your company's products or the business opportunity?

CA: I lead with the business opportunity based on the quality of the products. This way, people self-select into consumers or marketers on their own. When I lead with the products (and sometimes that is the right sequence) and a person decides to argue about the merits of what I'm presenting, I'm up against the wall in offering him a business opportunity based on a product he hasn't tried but is discounting. On the other hand, when I present the marketing history of this company, there is nothing to argue about; the statistics are facts. He may decide that he doesn't want to try his hand at NETWORK MARKETING but will usually try the product. Often, this same person will be so impressed with the personal benefits, he'll change his mind about networking this product. The risk in leading with the opportunity is people may get the false notion that you are minimizing the product, so I am careful to keep the two aspects intertwined in my presentation.

LE: I lead with my company's name. Second, is to briefly describe what the product will do for them. Third, I educate about the power of referral-based marketing and how they can participate.

JL: Very few companies have true leading-edge breakthrough products that are REALLY state of the art. In my case we are blessed and we REALLY DO, so it would be foolish not to lead with the product. How do I get my business builders? They come to me! Now, this is certainly not true in all companies, so it is a situational/ethical kind of question. If you have a "me too" or high tech company, you MUST lead with the opportunity. We have one of the best compensation plans in the industry, and I still lead with the product.

MR: I stay as far away from trying to know all the details of the products and sounding like a pharmacist. On the other hand, I stay as far away as possible from being a financial analyst. The power that drove my success was my relating to the products as a product that has stood the test of time over 20 years and won the respect and the referral of thousands of doctors. Blending the business conversation with the attitude that I have personally met the owners and the CEO, and I like how they treat people.

RS: Business Opportunity.

EW: John Kalench refers to this dilemma in his article in Upline Magazine (12/99), BEYOND CHICKEN AND EGG. My answer is: Don't show 'em the chicken or the egg. First tell them about farming itself. And farming, of course, is Network Marketing. We were attracted to Nikken, as were most distributors because of spectacular product results, so it's natural for us to promote the products right up front. In fact, I believe the validity of a network marketing opportunity rests upon the validity of the product line. Product results create passion beyond what just a compensation plan alone can. Passion creates a sense of mission that propels you up the company's recognition and income ladder. Nikken began with a product that was married to a compensation plan, not the other way around. Now, I'm just as passionate about the business opportunity as I am the product line, so I'm flexible when making a first contact. I would not have some of my best business builders today had I approached them first with the business. I saw a product need and met that first. It also helps that our products are so experiential and so quick that I can demonstrate results with anybody in 30 seconds. Quick results are definitely a benefit. When I'm prospecting, I'm fishing. The late Vince Spader, a Nikken Diamond, taught me the difference between fishing and hunting. A hunter pursues his prey with something the hunted doesn't want. A fisherman attracts his prey with something the fish wants. When fishing, my agenda isn't important. What is important is the fish's agenda. What I offer depends on what I think the fish is looking for. If it's a product need, I lead with products. If it's a financial need, I lead with the business. He or she may need the business desperately but they may never look at that until after a product experience. In fact, many who had no business need or interest or hated NETWORK MARKETING found themselves compelled to share the products, thus doing the business. It's great to be able to lead with either one, or both.

Rank the following traits in order of their importance in building a successful network marketing business: enthusiasm, persistence, knowledge, communication skills
CA: First is enthusiasm. Ignorance on fire is better than knowledge on ice. I want to be around happy, upbeat people. Second is communication skills. Lead from the heart and honestly care about people. To truly communicate isn't to spout fancy phrases but to stay in sync with the person you're talking to and really listen to his verbal and nonverbal messages. Third is to be persistent. Persistency for a good cause (to help with health or wealth) shows you are for real, that you are not just a reed in the wind, that you mean what you say. Last is knowledge. But people first need to be anchored and secure in the business arrangement before you teach or share specific knowledge. Smile with real warmth, listen, and "read" the other person. Be up front, and then sharing knowledge is a comfortable way to build business relations. Network marketing is all about building relationships, not making sales.
LE: Enthusiasm, communication (listening!), persistence, and knowledge.
JL: Persistence will forever be first; enthusiasm will forever be second; communication skills—basically listening and learning that God gave you two ears and one mouth—is next; and knowledge will forever be last!!!
MR: Enthusiasm, persistence, communication skills and knowledge. You don't have to know it all. Let the tools, tapes, brochures, and Websites educate.
RS: Persistence, communication skills, enthusiasm, knowledge.
EW: Enthusiasm: After observing hundreds of successes in network marketing, I've eliminated, as a common denominator, all factors (education, professional history, financial strength, gender, age, ethnicity, physical ability, appearance, religious preference, personality etc.) with the exception of DESIRE (enthusiasm). With it, one can succeed in spite of overwhelming handicaps. Without it, one is handicapped is spite of overwhelming ability. Persistence: There is no substitute. I've always believed that success in our business is simply a matter of doing the right things enough. I've seen many people do the right things but just not enough. It's like they've dug deep into a mountain looking for gold and abandoned the project six inches from the main vein. Knowledge: Some basic knowledge is necessary, but the Bible says, "My people perish for the lack of vision [not knowledge]." My advice is to get started with what you know now. The more you do what you know, the more you'll know what to do! Network marketing is the greatest on-the-job training industry, and you earn while you learn! Communication Skills: If you have them, fine. But even if you don't there are so many ways to effectively leverage the skills of others for your benefit, such as tapes, conference calls, three-way calls, public presentations, etc. My sponsor has often joked that a blind dog with a note in its mouth could build this business!

How long were you in network marketing before you saw your first four-figure commission check? Five-figure check?
CA: I saw one the first month in one company (after being in the industry for three years) but the company soon folded! In 1996 (six years experience in network marketing), I got a four-figure check in the second or third month and kept getting them this time. In about 26 months, my monthly checks jumped to five figures.
LE: My first exposure to the world of networking was in 1987. I played around for years. I saw my first four-figure monthly check in 1989. I saw my first five-figure week-

ly check in 1993. My income hit six figures per month in 1999, but I have not seen a six-figure "check" because I get paid weekly.

JL: Six months, nine months.

MR: It was eight months in my first experience before I earned a four-figure check. In my current experience, it was my first month. In the first five years, I never reached a five-figure check. In Life Force, I earned my first five-figure check in my tenth month and it doubled in just four months.

RS: Nine years, Nine months.

EW: We enrolled in August 1993 but didn't really get started until November of that year. Our first four-figure check was in March, four months later. Our first five-figure check was in September, 1995, our 22nd month of working the business. I should also point out, however, that our first network marketing experience, for six years in the 1980s, though not as productive, was a tremendous learning experience. So, really, when Nikken came along, we already had several years of experience. Nikken just turned out to be, as it has for many, the field in which the harvest of years of past effort has finally proved fruitful.

What's more important: the initial contact with a prospect or the follow-up?

CA: Both are necessary but you can't have the follow-up without the initial contact. Also, the initial contact sets the tone for the contacts to follow. If there is not a follow-up, you have wasted a precious opportunity and shortchanged the person you didn't re-contact. Hit the ball, run all the bases, and don't forget to slide into home plate if you want to be a player in this industry.

LE: With no initial contact there can be no follow-up. Chicken or the egg?

JL: The three most important words in NETWORK MARKETING are follow-up, follow-up, follow-up. It ain't gettin' 'em. It's keepin' 'em.

MR: Follow-up is everything!

RS: Both are equally important.

EW: I'm not sure which is more important because neither without the other is productive. The most difficult, by far, is the follow-up. Good seed, if not nourished, will die. But some mediocre seed, if properly cared for, can yield fruit. So, I would say the follow-up. Since success is a numbers game, if you're lousy at follow-up, just prospect that much more.

You've just recruited a promising new distributor. How do you help them get off to a good start? Or do you consider that the new distributor's responsibility?

CA: As a successful recruiter who just signed up a great prospect, now you immediately change hats and become his mentor/trainer. Use your personal system or the company's system to introduce him to the nuts and bolts to being a successful distributor, and start thatprocess within 24 hours of sign up. He is excited, full of dreams, and a little overwhelmed at all the new terms and concepts of your particular opportunity. Double team with him in person or on the phone as he selects the people to share this new opportunity with. Work three levels deep with him and his new group and teach him to do the same. Give him 30 to 90 days of your concentrated assistance and expect him to be a good beginner, not an expert, because he signed an application to become a distributor. Do, be, and say exactly what you want him to copy, but let him develop his own style and timetable. Have stewardship interviews in addition to helping him build his team so you and he are on the same business and personal wavelength. Recognize and commend his strengths rather than carping about his inevitable presentation errors. Be proud, not competitive, when he leaves you in his dust when he "gets it."

LE: I play a game. I want them to promise not to communicate this program with anybody. I want the names and phone numbers of the people they know. I want the list to be created with great speed, no time for thought, just the names.

JL: Getting a commitment—contracting to work with me a minimum of two years; goal setting or dream building—discovering their "why"; making out the contact list; reviewing what is in the starter kit; budgeting the money and time; suggesting books and tapes; creating a training schedule; and bonding.

MR: I want to talk to their 20 best people ASAP. I want to meet them at the head office, as this will sky-rocket their belief in the company. I want to do three-way calls with their prospects. In some cases I will help them out by giving them extra samples, brochures, etc., after I see proof of effort.

RS: I send them to my getting-started Website.

EW: A well-known hotel chain once advertised, "We don't train our people to be nice. We just hire nice people." In my business I don't feel it's my job to motivate people. I'm just looking for motivated people. A leader in our business says, "Find 'em and wind 'em and see who runs." I feel my job is to help that new distributor see the big picture of what our opportunity has to offer them. It's not about me getting them excited about what I want or what I'm excited about. If I can paint the picture as big as possible, as clear as possible, and, certainly, as accurately as possible, then I want to know if that new recruit sees him/herself in the picture and to what extent. I ask a lot of questions of a new distributor: What do you see in this picture for you? Where do you want to go and how quickly? Let's pretend my pen is a magic wand and I could wave it and poof you are a Royal Diamond!! What would that mean to you? What would you do that you can't now do? Where would you go? What would you buy? Who would you help? In order for me to responsibly sponsor someone, I need to know their why. Once I know that, then I can help outline a plan of how-to's that matches their why. If I don't find that out first, then we'll both be frustrated with expectations of each other that don't match up. Once we've established the why, then I'll plug them into the training infrastructure available: training materials, conference calls, special events, etc. They then need to show the initiative to access the support system and demonstrate the desire to run. If not, I'm not going to carry them. My new distributors know that I will work as hard for their success as they will, but I've learned long ago that wanting something for someone worse than they want it only leads to frustration.

How do you get your best leads?

CA: People lead me to people. I relax and take every opportunity I find to follow a lead. My best leads seem accidental. I just stay open and always have marketing materials in my purse or nearby in my home or car. Networking is an introducing and a sorting business to find the right people. Some say it's a numbers game. Well, it's true that you do have to kiss a lot of frogs to find the prince, but the whole process is a lot more fun if you like frogs/people. Others say you have to attract the right people. I think both ideas are correct. And many times I just look to heaven and say "thank you" for the good people that come my way.

LE: From the warm market. I love to ask my leads to give me the name and number of the most influential business person they know.

JL: Three-foot rule and referrals. I have built a kingdom with referrals.

MR: Referrals and trade shows.

RS: Bulk E-mail.

EW: The best leads are always what we typically call warm-market leads—those with whom the distributor already has established rapport and credibility. In our industry, a warm market includes those you know, and cold market is made up of those you don't know. However, I have found that some of those I know, including family, are quite cold. On the other hand, some that I have just met are incredibly warm. A key to me has been to just make friends with people. Show a genuine interest in them and they inevitably want to get to know who you are as well. Prospecting becomes a matter of lifestyle. I don't go out to prospect; I prospect because I'm out. There are many techniques for generating large numbers of leads—none of which I have used, though I have nothing against them. Keep in mind, it doesn't take that many good leaders to build a large organization. Most of our top distributors earn 75-80% of their income from three to five good legs. So, find a few good ones, help them find a few, then help those people.

I'm planning a big local meeting. What's the best way to fill the room?
CA: It sounds like a person is planning an introductory meeting for his business opportunity and hasn't had meetings in this area before. If he already has local leaders recruited, he needs two to four weeks lead time before having this meeting to generate a groundswell of enthusiasm for this major meeting. It is best to have many small cottage meetings before this big one so he and the local leaders should concentrate on these small group presentations first. Meanwhile, he schedules and advertises his meeting, promoting its special features or speakers and the uniqueness of this particular meeting. He needs to use the public media to do a feature on this upcoming meeting, get announcements carried in the business calendar section of paper where he will essentially be getting advertising for free, distribute flyers, get the local TV station to do a short piece on this upcoming event, and go to local service clubs, and personally invite its members. With his local leaders building a grassroots interest, these people become walking advertisements and build excitement for the coming meeting. If his budget allows, he can do spaced advertising leading up to the night before when he repeats his advertising pitch on a bigger ad with a specific reason why people should come to his meeting. I've seen this technique used without much media support and the room was packed because the new people were excited and brought their friends to this "important presentation."
LE: From an existing base of local distributors, I get a commitment for everybody to invite 10 people each, expecting each to get three to show up.
JL: Get your key people to commit to an agreed-upon number. Use the Lloyd math system: regardless of the committed number, HALVE IT, and you will be spot on—NEVER believe what you are told...never!
MR: Get your 10 best people to bring five each. Offer a free case of samples to the person who brings the most guests. Create excitement and enthusiasm for the event.
RS: I don't waste time doing meetings.
EW: Figure out how many you want to have. Get three times that number committed to come. Personal invitation is always the best. Running ads, posting flyers, sending direct mail announcements, etc. may produce some results, but nothing is as effective as individual invitations. In Nikken, unlike some companies, we've been blessed with tremendous crossline cooperation throughout North America. A large meeting in an area will be open to all distributors, thus increasing the chances of filling large meeting rooms. Rather than a sense of competition, the leaders have learned that what John Kennedy said years ago is true: "A rising tide raises all ships."

I need to generate a hundred leads within 60 days. What's my best strategy to achieve this?
CA: I like local radio talk shows for generating leads quickly. You pay a fee to go on the air and make your pitch in the form of an interview. Often, you end up with a tape of the

interview you can duplicate for more lead generation. Since time is a problem, try a newspaper advertising insert that is cleverly written and creates callers. You will need strong graphics and a catchy text to get people to call. Keep your message simple but address a basic need. See if you can get a newspaper interview for free exposure in your local newspaper. If you have a good name list, get on the phone and start calling. You won't have time for a mailing campaign, so just pick up the phone and put in the hours until you get your hundred leads. I suggest you do all these activities plus use your own warm-market contacts (all those people you were going to call but never got around to talking to). Now get more leads from the people who became your leads and you'll have more than 100 leads in 60 days.

LE: In this business if you sponsor two your first day and ask for them to provide two referrals each, the next day you would have four leads and so on, and so on:

2x2=4 leads
4x2=8 leads
8x2=16 leads
16x2= 32 leads
32x2= 64 leads
64x2= 128 leads

This is not rocket science. It does not take 60 days.

JL: 100 leads in 60 days is a cake walk. You could use the yellow pages, networking magazines, newspapers, one-on-one contact, and the three-foot rule. If you use tapes, hand out no less than 10 per day.

MR: Ask for referrals, ask for referrals, ask for referrals! Be sure to have your new recruits fill out their contact sheets and do the same for all their new people. Contact sheets should be a minimum of 50 people.

RS: Join ProSTEP.

EW: Anybody who has lived someplace for any amount of time at all can make a list of over 100 names. We teach distributors how to prioritize those names and take them through a simple evaluation process designed to give them enough information to either join our team, buy products, refer someone to us, or say no. Again, it's somewhat of a numbers game. Contact enough people to get 100 through the process and, in our experience, you'll have the foundation of a solid organization.

How many distributors must a person recruit each month to succeed in network marketing?

CA: The minimum number of distributors to recruit every month is one. It doesn't take a huge number of distributors personally sponsored to be successful, but it does take a consistent number of distributors adequately trained and supported to be successful. You set the example for your group by bringing one or more persons into the group and working them and their contacts until they are competent networkers. Just to quickly sign people up only to watch them "die" from being abandoned is cruel and will choke your business faster than anything else you could do.

LE: The answer varies with the style of the business. I was in a program once in which I sponsored 50 people and ended up with a downline of 300. In another program, I sponsored 30 people and had a downline that produced $20,000,000 of annual business. From another program, 12 people sponsored brought me a monthly volume of $100,000. In my current venture, I've sponsored seven in my first month and averaged just one new person per month after that. In 35 weeks, this group grew to 85,000 members.

JL: One per week and you will be financially free in five years. Do the math on that, and figure what five per week will do.

MR: One to three will get you there, provided you build friendships.

RS: 100: two will be leaders, 10 will do some recruiting, 20 will buy product, and the rest will do nothing.

EW: I guess that would depend somewhat on the particulars of their compensation plan and how success is defined. Our company has a special award for those who recruit two new first-level distributors for three consecutive months and not many win it. Also, people vary so much in their people equity. Some command tremendous influence and get people to join with a mere invitation. Others have to work much harder to achieve similar results. You recruit as many as it takes. Unfortunately, many that aspire to high levels want to know how little they have to do to get there. Those become the casualties along the trail. The ones who are determined to get there, no matter what, are the ones that make it.

Best tips for surviving rejection?

CA: Know why you are doing this business and believe in your ability to succeed. Do the basic activities of successful networkers: prospect, prospect, and prospect. Feed your mind by reading industry books and listening to tapes. Smile, and say to yourself, "NEXT!" Remember the law of the harvest: first you plant the seeds, then you water and pull the weeds (for as long as it takes), then you harvest the fruit at the end of the growing season, not before and certainly not the next day after planting the seeds in the ground.

LE: Once I understood my role of becoming a "messenger" of the information; the responsibility of accepting the information was passed on.

JL: No one can possibly reject you, they are rejecting what they really do not understand. It is all a question of timing. That is one reason why I promote using the tape system. The tape, not the person, is rejected. I NEVER promote "selling" the product or the opportunity, just the tape. It is pressure free.

MR: When you come from the heart and give away samples, you are not rejected. All you are doing is sharing an excellent product. Just know that not everything is for everybody at the same time.

RS: Prospect using the Internet.

EW: Many factors can cause a new distributor's enthusiasm level to fluctuate dramatically, rejection being the primary cause. What happens over time is that the distributors enthusiasm level will level out about where their belief level is. So what's the key? Build a rock-solid, unshakable belief in yourself, in others, in your company and products, and in the network marketing industry. Building your knowledge base strengthens your belief. So, read, listen to tapes, attend events, and plug in closely with leaders in your business that are where you aspire to be. Remember that rejection is usually rooted in ignorance. Will Rogers said that everybody is ignorant, just on different subjects. The problem is that many aren't content to just be ignorant, they're also opinionated about it. Finally, remember to never doubt your beliefs, and never believe your doubts.

Do you recommend that new distributors prospect close friends and family?

CA: Let the new distributor practice on someone else so his family doesn't see him when he is vulnerable. There is a lot for a new person to learn; don't add to his stress by letting him "struggle" in front of his family and friends. With a success underneath his belt and paychecks in the bank, he might start approaching a friend or two. Family members are usually the harshest critics of a new person in network marketing and the slowest to forget network marketing misadventures. Use the power of positive attraction with family and friends.

LE: Three-way calls are the best way to introduce to family and friends. An "expert" is defined as he who comes from farthest away.

JL: Never, never, never prospect family. Rule #1—Never! Save close friends until you have experienced some degree of success. They will ALWAYS wait and see, so why buck reality?

MR: Yes. Promote by giving samples as a gift, and do it in the spirit of giving not selling. If they don't use it, you still gave it and this will build a relationship with that person. Some will today, some won't today, some are waiting to hear the message. Focus on the good it can do them, not your check, and it will all work out.

RS: Only after they are making a profit and have a proven recruiting system.

EW: Sure, but be prepared for a wait-and-see approach from them. Some may join you right away but most will likely want to see your results down the road. Remember, even Jesus said that a prophet is without honor in his own country. Some close friends and family will only be convinced by a significant product experience, a sizable check, or some guy at work who puts in a good word for what you're doing that validates what you've been saying all along.

In five years I'll be....

CA: In five years I'll be grandfathered in my business for life. My group will literally wrap this globe with this special juice. I'll travel from country to country getting to know the wonderful people in my group. I won't have to lift a finger to receive the residual income we are planting seeds for all over the world. I'll be able to help some of the impoverished children of the world with my huge, extra income.

LE: I'll be living in fpur different homes in different corners of the world.

JL: I will have institutions throughout the country to benefit abused children. My business will be in 30 countries. My monthly income will be $500,000. I will have a house in England.

MR: I have a desire to spend some of my time in Canada, USA, and South Pacific embracing all the fun and adventures these beautiful vistas have to offer. Photography is my passion. In five years I will help 100 people personally find financial freedom. I will publish several books to help people see the good of network marketing like the friendships and caring that is developed by belonging to a great group of people. I will be an ambassador for network marketing from the heart, not from the wallet. My income will exceed a $500,000 a year, and I will use 20% a year to help others, and that will be fun.

RS: Fully retired and providing funds for my grandchildren to go to the schools of their choice.

EW: At the Royal Diamond level in our marketing plan. I will have helped at least five of our first-level distributors reach the Diamond level and will have at least 50 distributors in our group earning six-figure incomes. Ginger and I will be in good health, enjoying life with our children and six grandchildren. We will have a second home on a lake in the mountains that will serve as a family get-away and a missionary retreat. We will be making annual family expeditions to locations throughout the world for pleasure and missions-related projects. We will have a global business organization with leaders in all 50 states and at least a dozen foreign countries.

In ten years I'll be...
CA: In ten years I'll be doing all the charitable work I ever wanted to be doing and loving every minute of it. It will be time to attend high school and college graduations for grandchildren. I'll probably be a widow, but that will be okay. There will still be music I haven't heard and books I haven't read and walks I haven't taken—enough to last a lifetime.
LE: I'll be earning more money than my wife can spend!
JL: I will have institutions throughout the world to help abused children. My business will be in 80 countries. My monthly income will far exceed $1,000,000. I will have a third house in Australia.
MR: I will enjoy quality fishing trips to Alaska and fun cruises with the wonderful people I associate with in this business. I will earn whatever is fair for the service I have given. I feel that could be over $200,000 a month, but I am not in a panic to get it. It is my dream that many who prosper on this journey will travel together and fish together and sail the oceans of the world visiting ports of call together. After all, what is it all about if we cannot have great friends and family in our life doing fun things together.
RS: Fully retired and running my own charitable foundation to provide scholarships to private schools for children of single parents. Provide funds for my grandchildren to pursue any occupation that they choose without concern for their paycheck.
EW: A Nikken Royal Ambassador with six first-level Royal Diamonds and at least 20 Diamonds in our organization. We will meet regularly in exotic locations of the world for relaxation, celebration and planning. Our immediate family now includes 12 grandchildren who love to come to our ranch, mountain retreat, or Caribbean hide-away. Our estate is financially self-perpetuating through a strong, diversified portfolio. Our family focus is furthering our spiritual, social, and business values on a global basis with considerable time spent on each of the five continents where we have business interests.

What most motivates you in building your business?
CA: First, my own personal financial security; second, the joy I experience in seeing others regain their health and their financial freedom. Knowing that I can make a difference in this world through building networks around the world is the greatest service project ever. I love my business friends and rejoice in their success, and I know we are going to have an outstanding year!
LE: I get real, nice, warm-and-fuzzy feelings from seeing new people succeed in the business.
JL: Having a real honest opportunity to make this planet a better place by helping children be whole and complete, free from abuse. Having the opportunity to work with people who also desire to change the planet and supporting them to do so as they see fit. Knowing that I make a difference in so many lives and that my product WORKS.

MR: Freedom to do what I choose, when I choose. Originally I was upside down financially. So I needed a success story again. Now, I want to maintain and advance the prosperity I have started and have been so fortunate to receive. What I really enjoy is seeing others when the light goes on and their eyes light up and they really get it. Their action changes, their voices have power and they stand taller. It is fun to watch people support each other in the process of building their own businesses and become friends in the meantime. Helping others reach for their dreams is exciting and the lifestyle of time freedom is unexplainable.

RS: Proving it can be done.

EW: Our business has taken on the characteristics of a mission, cause, or crusade, not just a business. It's impossible to build a significant Nikken distributorship and not buy into the company ethic of wanting to impact world health on a large scale. Knowing that others are literally praying for the answers to physical and financial challenges, as we were, gives Ginger and I a sense of responsibility to continue to share what we have been so blessed to discover. In fact, we consider it a God-given mandate. I've also observed that it's common for people to pray for answers to life's problems, then not recognize the package the answer comes in. I almost missed this opportunity because of my initial skeptical, biased thinking. I know there are literally millions for whom this is an answer, but they just don't know it yet. I must tell as many as I can while I can.

How often do you read books and/or listen to or watch tapes for improving your business skills or knowledge?

CA: My office has a tape recorder, so does my kitchen and bathroom. My cars have a CD player and tape deck, so everywhere I go I have network marketing tapes/CDS ready to play. There are network marketing and motivational books in every room in my house. Some days I read, other days I play a tape or CD to stay focused on the attitudes and skills needed to be successful in this industry. The scriptures are part of my daily reading, also.

LE: About once a month. I do like audio tapes.

JL: VERY IMPORTANT QUESTION—EVERY DAY. Never let a day pass where you do not do so. The same goes for meditation and prayers—it is a daily, constant activity; it is the fuel that drives you to success. The degree of your success is directly related to how you adhere to what I just said. There are many tape series and books that I have read or listened to dozens of times. Each time I learn more. It is endless.

MR: Virtually every day, I never leave home without a book or a tape. If I am caught waiting in traffic or at an office waiting, I read. I believe it is 10 times easier to succeed if you learn from others.

RS: Weekly.

EW: Regularly. Several times a week, if not daily.

The most underrated activity in business is?

CA: Team building. Sometimes people call it duplicatio,n but that doesn't tell the whole story. You are building a strong business team that stretches downward and helps everyone on the team. They do the same, and you become a solid business organization. Team building requires vision, patience, dedication, and hard work. Training or skill building is only part of team building, but it is an important part.

LE: Getting on the phone and talking to people.

JL: Individual, one-on-one contact, and the three-foot rule, not high tech.

MR: I feel the most underrated activity in this industry is getting out and meeting people and making new friends. For me, the strongest contacts were made at trade shows and seminars.

An important point to remember is to not be in a "selling mode" but rather search for people who like what they do. People who smile and have a happy way about them. Fortunes are made in continued follow-up with good people that you like and are like-minded about this industry.

RS: Minimum daily achievements.

EW: Prospecting and talking to new people. I worked for years in the marketing department of a private school, focusing on recruitment and retention. The oldest, most established private schools or universities still put constant effort on building a large freshman class of new recruits. The same is true in our business. New people, distributors, or customers are the lifeblood of success.

The most overrated activity in business is?

CA: Using card decks. People don't buy or enter a business association with complete strangers; they want to work with people they know and enjoy being with. Too much money gets spent trying to entice strangers to look at your product/opportunity when they don't even know your name.

LE: Reinventing the wheel and creating a personal marketing presentation.

JL: Belief that the company understands what we do in the field. As long as they get the product delivered on time, we know how to do the rest. In other words WE are the company; and so many miss this point and rely way too much on the company to support them. "If it is going to be, it is up to me."

MR: Spending large amounts on advertising too fast. You need to test carefully and work in teams to co-op resources. I find that working any of the systems work, but I think you need to develop relationships to build leaders. Sponsoring a front line is overrated because it doesn't build teams. I've seen it both ways (building deep and building wide) and I feel width is good when done gradually. It's like building a bridge—build one pier at a time before you expand out from it. Just like a bridge, you build it for strength so that it will last a very long time. When done properly, just like a bridge, a strong organization will help you get where you want to go on your journey.

RS: Hype and convincing, not sorting.

EW: In our business, it's training. Look at fishing. No amount of reading fishing magazines, watching fishing programs, or attending fishing seminars will be as instructional as getting out and getting your line in the water. Nothing is more common than over-trained, under-productive sales people. Get out of the classrooms, boardrooms, and ballrooms, and get in the living rooms. GO FISHING!

If you had to start my business all over again, what would you do differently?

CA: I would not change a thing. I needed to learn from my fears and my mistakes. The law of opposition applies here. I would not appreciate my present success if the business had been easy and without challenges. Mistakes mean you are alive and trying to reach your goals, and mistakes make great teachers. In a perfect world, I would have had more self-confidence, kept better financial records, and not spent money advertising in magazines and newspapers. Instead, I would have told prospects what I know in a more simple, straightforward style.

LE: Had a little more money, safety cushion, in the bank.

JL: Not too much. I was blessed with the best upline sponsor in the world, Johnny Keller—one of the true leaders in NETWORK MARKETING. I simply listened to him and followed his advice. If anything, I would have mailed out ten times more tapes than I did!

MR: Initially I put a few people in my organization for free and this only creates a welfare mentality. I now only sponsor people when they are ready to build. That is my experience. Also I would have been less competitive in spirit. I was trying to compete, but when I took the focus off of myself in the equation for success, I made stronger alliances faster.

RS: I wouldn't change anything, it has been a learning experience.

EW: Contact the names on my chicken list sooner. Some of the people you think wouldn't be interested or don't need a home-based business will see the opportunity quicker than many who need it desperately. Coming from a ministry background, I spend a lot of energy trying to help people who didn't want help as bad as I wanted it for them. I would simply talk to more people sooner and find more leaders.

What was your worst business decision?

CA: Once I put up two billboards to advertise a product no one had ever heard of. That was an expensive lesson I got zero calls from that ad.

LE: Faking it before I made it.

JL: I went to Europe to help set up a NETWORK MARKETING company without first checking out the investors who proved to have no integrity. ALWAYS know who you are working with. KNOW your company, do your homework, and go with your gut!

MR: Spending money (thousands) on a person who had not proven themselves as a leader. I was getting caught up in what was going to happen, not what was happening. Now I let people prove their ability before I get involved.

RS: Spent money on prospecting tools that had become obsolete, i.e. cassette tapes and video tapes.

EW: Trying to manage my group at times, rather that staying creative, constantly bringing in new people, and leading by example.

What was your best business decision?

CA: On a shoestring budget, I sent product overseas to women I'd only spoken to on the phone once. The cost of the product and international shipping set me back some serious grocery money. This lady was a clinical nutritionist and had worked with a famous scientist making dietary supplements, so I was intimidated by her experience. She fell in love with the product and has since built a huge international group. We are great friends and team builders.

LE: Joined a program for the personal value of the product first. Promoted the program second.

JL: Creating a close personal relationship with my upline sponsor, Johnny Keller. Following his wisdom and the advice that wisdom created. It is a business of relationships, go with that energy and you will always succeed!

MR: My best decision was reinvesting resources in the hands of the people that had more contacts than I did. Primarily this was done in support of fly-ins to have people visit the company. This has been very successful for all concerned.

RS: To get involved in SFI.

EW: Signing up! Agreeing to evaluate some information as a courtesy gesture to my eventual sponsor, Chuck Branham. Also, taking the initiative to make the first contact with the individuals who are now my key leaders.

What do you consider to be the main keys of your success?

CA: The key ingredients for my success are the integrity of the products I represent, the seamless marketing plan which is already in place in most areas of the world, and go-getter uplines and downline partners who are not afraid to take risks and work hard. We believe in what we are doing and are the strongest group in the company. I go the extra mile for our group and they do the same for each other. We are a powerful, global team because we support each other and believe in our mission to get this product all over the world. The great pay we receive keeps people excited and motivated to work harder.

LE: To be accessible to the organization.

JL: Using a low-key, non-hype approach, not desiring to "change" people or what they want, finding out what they want and helping them attain it, NEVER quitting, staying in touch with my creator, meditating and praying daily, and keeping physically fit.

MR: Consistent, persistent focus on what you want to be the future of your life.

RS: Persistence; I refused to quit!

EW: Several factors come to mind quickly. I saw the big picture early on and have worked to develop the ability to help others, in turn, expand their vision, and see the opportunity on a large scale. I genuinely like people and enjoy creating rapport with a wide variety of people, inspiring them to fulfill their potential. I made a decision to do the business, not try to do it. It was obvious that it could be done others had already done it. So, if it could be done, I reasoned I could do it. And, if I could, then I should. The support and participation of my wife Ginger and my children has been a great blessing. We've maintained a healthy balance of work and fun, making the journey enjoyable.

What's your success philosophy?

CA: To be successful, a person has to believe that he/she is worthy of success (otherwise, people push success away from themselves). Then a person needs to be a realist and see what is going on around him. For example, people are sick and turning to alternative health for answers, spending billions of dollars each year. Find a need and fill it. In my case, I became an independent distributor for a juice that made a difference in my health and helps others. Persevere against all odds and know in your heart that you're right. My company was only days old and most companies fail in the first one to two years. I took a huge risk. You will achieve success in proportion to the success you help others achieve. Many in my group are now more successful than I am. It was a great experience to help them succeed. A truly successful person is more than just wealthy; he/she is a decent human being.

LE: "What you see, is what you get."

JL: Never compromise; be honest with others but especially with yourself. Ignore what your "brain" says and always go with your heart and gut. Never come from greed or lack but from abundance.

MR: Be in a state of gratitude for all that God has given you and approach others with a kind and giving spirit. Be a giver not a taker. Focus on the dream of others and ask them for a commitment. My success rule is "Treat others better than you ever EXPECT to be treated."

RS: Persistence.

EW: Jesus told his followers "If you want to be great, become the servant of all." True success comes as a result of rendering service to others, not at their expense. You must literally serve your way to the top.

What about you has changed the most since finding success in business?

CA: I am more calm and confident inside and more sincere outside. My intensity made others nervous. My view of the world has changed. I no longer want to accumulate more possessions but am content with what I have. Seems like getting rid of insecurities stripped me of competitiveness. So I like the person I have become as a result of business success.

LE: I really enjoy being debt free.

JL: Very little. I am the same now as I was before. I believe that is the key to success. I ALWAYS saw myself successful even when I had nothing. I believed in myself; I had the vision of success; I set my goals and went out and made them a reality. The thing that has changed the most is I have more to give away than I ever thought possible. Giving is so wonderful; I love to give.

MR: I believe the big change came in my life just before the money did. I had to change my attitude. When I began to build with a sense of caring about people, a flow of success started. Now that the money is here, I feel more energetic. It feels great to put your faith behind a project and see it blossom. I am fulfilled to be able to help others. I am able to rekindle dreams and have an expanded vision for the future. It is fun to buy a friend dinner again. I also see a real change in my desire and focus for better health through exercise.

RS: Financial peace of mind.

EW: My confidence level is higher. My vision is bigger. My life's mission and purpose is clearer and I'm more focused in my pursuit of it. My resolve is stronger.

What is the legacy you hope to leave?

CA: I hope to leave hundreds of thousands of people around the world happier and in better health because of the collective efforts of our group. I hope to invest my income wisely to benefit children's health here in the United States.

LE: If I can become successful in this business, anybody can do it.

JL: The more you give, the more you will receive. Find your passion and live it to the fullest. Live life with passion, never regret one moment. Always know that every cloud has a silver lining.

MR: I wish to be remembered as a person who was creative and shared a vision of a bigger life. Someone who played it to the fullest and set an example that a life without goals is nothing at all. My legacy will be that of a teacher and the lesson is that "LIFE IS WHAT YOU MAKE OF IT."

RS: Loving husband, father, grandfather, and great-grandfather. I have helped thousands achieve their financial dreams.

EW: As one who loved God, loved his family, lived in peace, and bettered the lives of all he touched. The Bible says "A good man leaves an inheritance for his children's children." May my descendants have a stronger platform of faith and fortune from which to carry out their life's purpose because I lived.

Joe Brennan

Age: 32

Family: Brenda (Wife), 29; Jessica (Daughter), 2

Highest Education: High school

Year Started Business: 1996

Type Of Business: Internet services

Market: Opportunity seekers and business owners

Number Of Employees: Six

Best Month (Gross Revenues): $72,846

Hours Worked Per Week During Start-Up: 17

Hours Worked Per Week Now: Eight to 12

Favorite Business Magazines: No time to read

Relaxes By: Playing golf

Keeps In Shape By: Playing golf

Favorite Part Of Job: Opening email to watch the orders flow in and getting calls from people that we helped, thanking us for our service.

Least Favorite Part Of Job: Bookkeeping

Companies Admired: Network Solutions, Lycos, eBay, Amazon.com

The Person Who Most Influenced Your Life: "Mother and Father always instilled in me that 'I can become whatever I want as long as I put my mind to it.' Ain't that the truth."

Heroes: "Again Mom and Dad! Always taught my sisters and me not to work on your dreams but to work with what you have."

Special Accomplishments: A few Website design awards

Favorite Quotes: It is from my failures that I succeed.—Michael Jordan, You can't achieve the 'goal' if you never take the shot.—Wayne Gretzky, It can only become what "you" make of it.—Joe Brennan

Contact Joe At: (919) 854-5544

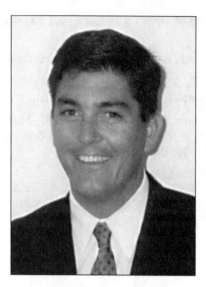

Jim Lewis

Age: 36

Family: Janine (Wife); Children: Kaylie, 7; Taylor, 4

Highest Education: Bachelor's in business administration

Year Started Business: Started network marketing in November 1993; in June of 1995, he started with his current company, ProSTEP, and began his consulting business called Wealth Builders International

Type Of Business: Consultant and trainer to the network marketing community

Market: Anyone involved with a network marketing, network marketing or home-based business program

Number Of Employees: None

Best Month (Gross Revenues): $53,000

Hours Worked Per Week During Start-Up: 60+ hours a week

Hours Worked Per Week Now: About 40 hours a week

Favorite Business Magazines: Robb Report, Success, Network Marketing Lifestyle

Favorite Authors: Dan Kennedy, Napoleon Hill, Og Mandino

Relaxes By: Running, working out, and riding his Jet Ski or Dirt Bike

Keeps In Shape By: Running three to four times per week and working out three times per week

Favorite Part Of Job: "I love talking to new people and watching them blossom and grow as they realize all that is possible with their business. It's an incredible awakening! I am in the people-growing business and take great pride in being able to be a catalyst to provide the tools, coaching, inspiration, and to nudge someone in the right direction until they become successful on their own terms! I love the successes that only this business can produce!"

Least Favorite Part Of Job: "Listening to the whiners and complainers who blame everybody and everything but themselves. There is very little you can do for people with a negative attitude. People who truly have a dream can change their own attitudes and turn their whole lives around. I can be there in the background coaching and encouraging and helping people build their businesses and make their dreams become a reality but I can't change an 'attitude'! That's frustrating!"

Companies Admired: ProSTEP Inc, EAS Nutritional, and Amazon.com

The Person Who Most Influenced Your Life: His father. "He never judged me or my business and supported me when I left behind a corporate career to pursue network marketing fulltime."

Heroes: "My father. He is an incredible, level-headed guy and a smart businessman. He taught me to look at business decisions from all perspectives and to apply logic and think through all possible consequences. Also, Andy Hummel, my partner. What an incredible mentor and friend he has been. He helped me to dream big and, more importantly, to enjoy the ride."

Special Accomplishments: "Together with my partner, Andy Hummel, we have built the #1 organization in ProSTEP. We've also produced many ProStep leaders and top earners."

Favorite Quotes: I will persist until I succeed.—Og Mandino, All our dreams can come true - if we have the courage to pursue them.—Walt Disney, Whether you think you can or think you can't, you are right.—Henry Ford

Contact Jim At: (888) MLM-PROS

David Seitz

Family: Wife, Joann (26); twin girls, Haylee & Zoey (6)

Highest Education: High School

Year Started Business: 1998

Type of Business: Internet Marketing and development including the world of affiliate marketing.

Market: We target a global audience both on and offline, from marketing and consulting to custom Internet development.

Number Of Employees: 5

Best Month (Gross Revenues): $25,000

Hours Worked Per Week During Start-Up: 60+

Hours Worked Per Week Now: "It's to the point now where I don't consider our business work so I do not keep track of time. When work becomes fun, you know you have found gold."

Favorite Business Magazines: Interactive week, Six-Figure Income, Internet World

Relaxes By: Spending time with his wife and children. "We are very close, and it's not uncommon to just pick up and go together on a moment's notice. I feed off them, and just being around them can make any dull day great. I also recently picked up a couple new toys including a dual sport motorcycle and a 4x4 so you may find me motoring through the woods on a regular basis. It's great to just get away from the digital world every now and then."

Keeps In Shape By: Off-road motorcycling, mountain biking.

Favorite Part Of Business: "I would have to say the favorite part of my job is when I finally see one of our ideas start to bloom and turn into a product. From idea to global market, it's a great feeling. I also enjoy helping our affiliates create real revenue online. I have seen dozens of people go from living from paycheck to paycheck to starting their own home-based business via the Internet. It's a powerful feeling knowing you helped change someone's life!"

Least Favorite Part Of Business: Anything repetitive. "There is a certain redundancy when you are using the Internet for most of your marketing."

Companies Admired: Dell, America Online, AllAdvantage.

People Who Most Influenced Your Life: "My wife Joann. I would not be where I am today if it were not for her. She is my true soulmate and best friend."

Special Accomplishments: "We have received several product awards for the development of Snapshot Spy: Snapshotspy.com and several achievement awards for our online marketing publication. Hopefully there will be many more in the future."

Best Thing About Being Self-Employed: "The freedom to do whatever we want whenever we want without being tied to a time clock. I can run our business from anywhere in the world as long as I can get a laptop connected to a phone or satellite signal."

Contact David At: 570-283-9368

David publishes A Helping Hand online. Readers can pick up a free subscription at www.helpinghand-newsletter.com.

Ron Wade

Age: 29

Family: DeAnn (wife), 27; Sons: Gage, 8; and Britt, 3

Highest Education: Bachelor's degree

Year Started Business: 1997

Type Of Business: Test and balance

Market: Mechanical contractors

Number Of Employees: None

Best Month (Gross Revenues): $40,000

Hours Worked Per Week During Start-Up: "I only receive work by bids, so it takes some time to build up a job list. I probably only worked 20 to 25 hours a week in the beginning because business was slow."

Hours Worked Per Week Now: "I currently work about 60 to 70 hours a week. But my work is in construction, so it's pretty much feast or famine. I still can go three or four weeks at a time with no work."

Favorite Business Books And Authors: Self-help books, personal finance books, and the Bible

Relaxes By: "I like to sit in my swing in the backyard after a hard day's work and watch my boys play."

Keeps In Shape By: Working out, running, and playing basketball

Favorite Part Of Job: Sending out the invoices

Least Favorite Part Of Job: "Much of my job involves troubleshooting problems, and it can be extremely frustrating to spend several days on a problem and still not have it resolved."

Companies Admired: Microsoft and Amazon.com

The Person Who Most Influenced Your Life: Jesus Christ

Heroes: "Jesus Christ because he is who he is."

Favorite Quotes: It is finished!—Jesus Christ; I like it a lot.—Dumb & Dumber; I firmly believe that any man's finest hour, the greatest fulfillment of all that he holds dear, is the moment when he has worked his heart out in a good cause and lies exhausted on the field of battle–victorious.—Vince Lombardi

Contact Ron At: (318) 325-5754

Irvin Widmer

Age: 55

Family: "I am a single parent with four wonderful, successful children. My son Mickey (27) is an accomplished musician and has made several CD's. Debi (23) is very successful in the restaurant business. Matthew (18) is about to graduate from a prominent Music and Drama college in New York City, and Nancy (17) is graduating from high school this year. I am very proud of them and all their accomplishments."

Highest Education: High school

Year Started Business: Current opportunity since June 1999

Type Of Business: Irv runs an Internet-related business in which he markets courses and information on how to use computers, build Websites, and advertise on the Internet. He also markets courses about the Internet itself.

Market: Any person in the world who has a computer, as well as the many people who do not have a computer but go online (at the library, etc.) to learn the information and education that we provide. "We make our product available (by way of the Internet) in 10 seconds to any person in the world."

Number Of Employees: One part-time employee

Best Month (Gross Revenues): $65,000

Hours Worked Per Week During Start-Up: 10 to15 hours a week

Hours Worked Per Week Now: "My business currently could run without me. But, because I love what I do, I continue to work 30 to 60 hours per week."

Favorite Business Magazine: Robb Report

Favorite Business Books And Authors: Think and Grow Rich and The Science of Getting Rich

Relaxes By: "I disappear to the coast or to the lake."

Keeps In Shape By: Going to the health club at least three times a week

Favorite Part Of Job: Making three-way calls with his team players

Least Favorite Part Of Job: "Dealing with the people who want to get rich in a week."

Companies Admired: Skybiz.com and Microsoft.

The Person Who Most Influenced Your Life: "My mother. She always said: 'Irvin, you can do or be anything you want to do or be.'"

Heroes: "There are two people that I admire greatly, and from whom I have learned a lot: Ronald Reagan and J. Douglas Edwards, who was, in my opinion, the greatest sales trainer that ever existed."

Special Accomplishments: Honored as the #5 earner of a Fortune 500, Inc. company, as well as being selected to be a corporate trainer for that company; also honored as a top earner in his current Internet-related business

Favorite Quotes: If you keep doing what you have always done, you will keep getting what you have always gotten—unknown; If you shoot for nothing, you will hit it every time.—unknown; Don't let the fear of striking out keep you from swinging.—Babe Ruth

Contact Irv At: (503) 463-0122

Tom Wood

Age: 35

Family: Single

Highest Education: Bachelor's of Science

Year Started Business: 1995 TheDuplicator.com, 1998 Pre-Paid Legal Services

Type Of Business: Network Marketing (PPL), Online Training (TheDuplicator.com)

Market: Anyone who lives under the U.S. or Canadian legal system (PPL); anyone in the world who wants to make more money in network marketing (TheDuplicator.com)

Number Of Employees: None

Best Month (Gross Revenues): "More than some years I had!"

Hours Worked Per Week During Start-Up: 70

Hours Worked Per Week Now: 40

Favorite Business Magazines: Upline, Business 2.0, Fast Company

Favorite Business Books And Authors: Atlas Shrugged—Ayn Rand, Unlimited Power—Tony Robbins, Think and Grow Rich—Napoleon Hill

Relaxes By: "I love to travel and learn. Any kind of adventure travel is actually relaxing to me. I also go to seminars, read books, attend classes, and write in my journal to renew and refresh myself."

Keeps In Shape By: Working out four to five times per week, running, playing tennis, golfing, hiking, and skiing

Favorite Part Of Job: Interacting with people. "I love discovering their stories and seeing their passion to have more in their lives."

Least Favorite Part Of Job: Paperwork. "If there is one guy who hates to dot the i's and cross the t's, it's me!"

Companies Admired: TheDuplicator.com, Pre-Paid Legal Services Inc., Microsoft

The Person Who Most Influenced Your Life: "My father was the most incredibly supportive, positive, happy person I have ever known. He always let me know that it was OK to fail, as long as I failed giving my best."

Heroes: His mother—" The most giving person I've ever known. The world is less without her." Abraham Lincoln—"He fought for freedom for all people in the Civil War." Thomas Jefferson—"He wrote the Declaration of Independence."

Special Accomplishments: Gold Executive Director, Gold Ring earner in Pre-Paid Legal

Favorite Quotes: "Every man dies. Not every man truly lives."—Mel Gibson in Braveheart

Contact Tom At: (954) 565-5585

The Interviews

Joe Brennan
(JB)

Jim Lewis
(JL)

David Seitz
(DS)

Ron Wade
(RW)

Irvin Widmer
(IW)

Tom Wood
(TW)

GETTING STARTED:

I'm starting a home business next month. I have a maximum of $3,000 in start-up capital. Where should I invest it?

JB: You need to be able to find something that offers a low investment, from $300 to $1,500. Then take the remaining $1,500 and nurture it with as much advertising as it will buy.

JL: I am assuming that you are starting a home-based, network-marketing business. Start by purchasing a premier membership in ProSTEP. This package will not only give you 1,050 leads a month, but will give you an incredible number of Internet and phone-related marketing tools as part of the package price. Lease an adequate computer and get yourself a good Internet access connection. Purchase a small amount of start-up product to retail, but don't spend more than 25% of your budget on this. Put the rest into additional advertising.

DS: I would suggest investing the bare minimum needed to run and market your business until you are generating revenue. Many businesses fail because they purchase too many "needless" materials and services. If you have a real, quality product or service, I would recommend investing as much as you can afford into marketing; revenue will then naturally flow in.

RW: With only $3,000 to start off with, I would either acquire a line of credit at the bank, or save up some more money before I took the leap of faith. Another option would be to begin a part-time business and continue working your job until your company can support you.

IW: In the business opportunity that I am in, the start up cost is $110.00. So the only continued monthly expense that I have is my telephone bill. I would keep the money liquid in order to pay my phone bills until I was making a profit.

TW: Network marketing, period. There is no other way I know of for the average person to develop significant passive income with such little start-up capital.

I've just started a home business. My spouse has given me six months to make it work. Any advice?

JB: You need a Website! With only six months to make it work, you need to be able to tell as many people as possible that you're in business, what you offer, and why they need it from your company. The Internet is the quickest, cheapest way to do so. Even small, local businesses need Websites. A restaurant can display indoor and outdoor pictures of the restaurant, menus, catering prices, or e-mail for future reservations. A painter or carpenter can show before and after pictures of his or her work. A Website is a "24-hour Full-Color Brochure" for any business. For the first year, a Website will cost less than $3 per day—that's full design, monthly fees, and domain name for less than $3 per day. It's the most affordable advertising anywhere. Then local businesses can just add a brief line under their phone number in all the existing advertising that they do that says, "View our 24-hour Color Brochure by visiting www.their-domain-name.com."

JL: In my first six months after I quit my job, I locked myself in a room for 16 hours a day, and in three months I replaced my salaried income. Today, I have a rock-solid business going. Being totally committed and working really hard is key.

DS: Again, I am leaning toward marketing. As long as you have a solid product or service, you should focus on marketing. The more eyes you get in front of the product/service, the better. The Internet offers a huge marketing opportunity where you can really stretch your dollars. Remember, marketing is an ongoing task. Making it work in six months is possible, but "keeping" it working will be a regular part of your business.

RW: Yes. I have failed at a couple of other businesses. It was the third company that I started that was finally successful. There is no such thing as a six-month trial period to make it work. In both of the failed companies, I knew when it was time to get out. It was when I was totally broke and all of my lines of credit were maxed out. The bottom line is this: starting a company will require that you step out of your comfort zone. There is no safety net when you're out on your own. I would suggest not setting a six-month limit. Instead, both of you need to realize that you WILL BE OUT OF YOUR COMFORT ZONE in the beginning of any new business, and stick with it as long as you possibly can take it. Then if it doesn't work out, decide to try a different route together. Just remember, your limit may not be the same as that of your spouse. So, don't push your spouse too far.

IW: If I were in those circumstances, I would set a goal for where I wanted to be in six months, and then I would make three-way calls with my upline every minute that I could fit in until I reached my goal. Be consistent; don't let "No" slow you down, and never give up until you get there.

TW: Negotiate with your spouse for a one-year limit. Businesses take time to make a profit. If you want to make an income right away, get a job. But if you spend 15 to 20 hours a week building a business, you should expect to break even in a year. I'm serious. The people who tell you they are making $10,000 per month in the first three months have been in business for years before they started their new venture. They already have the contacts and the training it takes to succeed. It might take some time for you to make it, but once you do, you will be forever transformed. You'll have the confidence to do just about anything.

They say it takes money to make money. Should I try to get a small-business loan for my start-up capital or just try to get by with my own limited finances?

JB: It really is up to what you are comfortable with. The thing to do is never give up on your determination to succeed. Henry Ford of the Ford Motor Company had 14 prior bankruptcies before the Ford Motor Company. Donald Trump claimed bankruptcy, Sharon Stone... and the list goes on. Michael Jordan was cut from the high school basketball team because the coach said he wasn't good enough. Can you see the pattern? They all had the determination to forge forward, believe in themselves, and never give up!

JL: If you have the $3,000 in start-up capital, use that for start up and reinvest your checks when they come in. My preference would be to have an available credit line to fall back on. It doesn't take much money to start up a viable network marketing business!

DS: The last thing I would recommend to a start up is a loan! Use a loan as an absolute last resort. True it takes money to make money, but it also takes resources. The more people you come in contact with and network with, the better off you are. Partner up with other businesses and people and create as many win/win situations as you can to save money.

RW: I would definitely get a loan for start up. I would not have made it without one.

IW: Depending on the amount of capital needed, I would recommend getting by without borrowing. For example, the opportunity I am involved in only takes $110 to get started, and, hopefully, one could come up with that without borrowing.

TW: It doesn't matter how you do it; just don't be insufficiently financed. It's actually not about the money. It's about the desire. If you want freedom bad enough, if you are sick and tired of your job, your boss, your situation, you will find a way to get exactly what you need to make it in your own business. Success in business doesn't go to the one with the most money, the most education, or the most contacts. It goes to the one with the most heart.

Do you consider yourself an early adopter of new technology?

JL: Yes, I would say so. We've been using the Internet for network marketing for over three years. ProStep aggressively uses all the Internet technologies and tools available.

DS: Absolutely. We have been online since the early 90's and try to keep up with new technology.

RW: Yes.

IW: Yes.

TW: Yes.

If you use a toll-free phone number, what is your primary use for it?

JB: The sole purpose is to add credibility to my business.

JL: We primarily use toll-free numbers as a means of connecting people to our voice mail box information system.

IW: Very selectively. I give it out once in a while. I call a prospect, and if they need to call me back with any questions before the scheduled follow-up call, I give it to them. I don't put it on my cards.

How do you use voice mail?

JL: Our voice mail system provides people with initial information about us and our company. It patiently gives the same information over and over again! It is a good way to sort out people who are not interested. This leaves us more time to spend with the people who ARE interested!

DS: Support and 24-hour lead generation.

RW: Since I am the only employee, my voice mail is my lifeline.

IW: I want my people to always be able to get in contact with me. If I am on another line, they can use my voice mail to leave a message.

Describe your computer system and how you use computers in your business.

JB: A Windows 98, 550 MHz system with a 13GB hard drive, 256MB RAM, a scanner, and a digital camera.

JL: I have a Gateway 700 with 27GB hard drive. I have a cable connection, scanner, and laser printer. I'm shopping for a digital camera.

DS: We have several newer Pentium computers on an in-house network. Details are too numerous to mention here.

Technology Utilized

	Fax*	Fax-on-Demand	Toll-Free	Voice Mail	Computer	Email	Internet	Website	Email Auto-Responders
Joe Brennan	✓	✓	✓	✓	✓	✓	✓	✓	✓
Jim Lewis	✓	✓	✓	✓	✓	✓	✓	✓	✓
David Seitz	✓	✓	✓	✓	✓	✓	✓	✓	
Ron Wade	✓		✓	✓	✓	✓	✓	✓	
Jim Lewis	✓	✓	✓	✓	✓	✓	✓	✓	
Irv Widmer	✓	✓	✓	✓	✓	✓	✓	✓	
Tom Wood	✓	✓		✓	✓	✓	✓	✓	✓

* Dedicated fax line

RW: I have a laptop and printer with a backup LS-120 drive for all my files. I use the computer to generate the reports that I must turn in to the engineers.
IW: I use an IBM-compatible machine. I rely heavily on the computer for e-mailing information. I also use it for my Internet business.
TW: Everything...!

What software do you consider in the "must-have" category?
JB: QuickBooks Pro.
JL: There are a few software programs I consider necessary to my network marketing business. The first is a good e-mail program, Eudora Pro (www.eudora.com). A powerful word processor, spreadsheet program and database is also necessary. Microsoft Office includes Word, Excel, and Access. I actually use Microsoft Works for my database program because it's smaller and easier to use than Access. Another program that is indispensable to me is World Merge. This handy program merges names and e-mail addresses into a message and delivers the message to hundreds or thousands of people at a time. It is a great way to keep in touch with your downline!
DS: A contact database is a must have. We use Microsoft Outlook because of its wide configuration possibilities and the large volume of e-mail we receive. Any software to help automate your marketing is also another high priority. Let your computer do as much of the work as possible...that's what it's for!
RW: Microsoft Office, QuickBooks, and TurboTax
IW: I consider a good e-mail program essential. I recommend Microsoft Outlook for its easy-to-use e-mail communication and address book capabilities. This software makes it easy for me to keep in touch with my (approx. 45,000) customer base associates, usually on a daily basis.
TW: E-mail! Contact is king in business.

What other "techno-toys" do you use in your business?
JB: Cellular phone, laptop, Website
JL: The only techno-toy I use is the cell phone, and I even restrict that to outbound calls only.
DS: Cell phone, laptop.
RW: I have a cell phone.
IW: I use a cell phone, a palm top, and a portable computer.
TW: Cell phone, Palm Pilot, and a laptop.

If you use the World Wide Web, name up to five personal favorite business URL's our readers can benefit from:
JB: iypdirect.com, hostit2000.com, and interwebclassifieds.com/
JL: You can find lots of great information about the network marketing industry at www.mlmpros.com. Eudora Pro, www.eudora.com, is one of the best e-mail management packages available. And, of course, I would be remiss if I didn't mention our free leads site at www.freeleads.com/team/Rockett.
DS: www.pricewatch.com, www.entrepreneurmag.com, www.associatesearch.com, www.sixfigureincome.com, www.helpinghand-newsletter.com of course!
IW: www.skyboom.com/Irv. Another site is www.globalmetric.com/time. I use this to find what time it is in each of the 60+ countries in which I do business.
TW: www.theduplicator.com, www.paypal.com, and www.gator.com

Of all the technology you use, rank your top three:

JB: Website, computer, and e-mail.

JL: The telephone for personal networking and contact; telephone technologies, such as voice mail boxes, #800 numbers, and conference calls; and computers as indispensable tools for organizing, e-mail contact, and Internet technologies.

DS: Internet, e-mail, and phone.

RW: Computer, cell phone, and pager.

IW: Computer, Palm Top, and cell phone.

TW: Internet, Internet, Internet.

Do you market on the Internet?

JB: A must—advertising, follow up, tracking sales, and receiving orders.

JL: Our website, www.freeleads.com/team/Rockett, lets people know about our company, our products, and our network-marketing compensation plan. By the time people go through it, they have a really good idea about whether or not they are interested. We have some people just signing up, others call or e-mail us for more information. It really works well for us.

DS: We use the Internet extensively. Everything from direct e-mail and search engine marketing to viral and affiliate marketing.

RW: No.

IW: Yes, I have a Website. The Internet is the wave of the present and the future.

TW: E-mail (tomwood@tomwood.net), word-of-mouth (TheDuplicator.com), and search engines.

Approximately what percentage of your sales originate from this marketing?

JB: 80%.

JL: The percentage of the sales from Internet marketing is growing steadily, more than other methods. More of our leads are coming from the Internet. Once people get onto the Internet, they want to do business that way.

DS: 90%.

IW: Most all of my business is handled through the media of the Internet. My business is selling education on the World Wide Web.

TW: 50%.

Do you use direct mail? If YES...in what way?

JB: Yes, direct e-mail lists

JL: We had a special postcard designed and printed; we send this out to our various lists on a regular schedule. This results in people going to the #800 number or to our Website for more information.

DS: Yes, we use direct postcard mailings and personalized letters.

Approximately what percentage of your sales originate from this marketing?

JB: 20%.

DS: 5%.

Do you use print media? If YES...in what way?
JB: Yes, classifieds in newspapers.
JL: We regularly run ads ourselves and co-op ads with our downline. The ads are targeted to those who already have network marketing businesses but need a regular source of free qualified leads.
DS: Yes, we place magazine advertising and use card decks.

Approximately what percentage of your sales originate from this marketing?
JB: 20%.
JL: Most of our leads come from the Internet.
DS: 5%.

Do you use radio and/or TV advertising? If YES...in what way?
DS: Not at the moment, but we are developing a radio and television marketing plan.
IW: We use radio to do talk shows to let people know what we do.

Approximately what percentage of your sales originate from this marketing?
IW: Not too much, maybe 5% to 10%.

What other kinds of marketing do you utilize?
JL: We use fax broadcasting.
DS: Word-of-mouth and marketing to our current customers.
RW: I get all of my work through the hard bid process. Lowest bidder gets the job.
IW: Mostly warm market, and then the warm market of the people who join my business with me.
TW: Word of mouth, about 50% of my referrals.

Do you recommend using a toll-free number in advertising? Why or why not?
JB: Yes, adds huge amount of credibility and people are much more inclined to ask questions if they see a toll-free number.
JL: I absolutely recommend using a toll-free number. People are reluctant to call a regular number when they don't know what to expect. A toll-free number removes any anxiety about that. The idea is to make it as easy and painless as possible for people to get in touch with you.
RW: I make my toll-free number available to all of my customers, even my local ones.
IW: I don't. The reason being, if someone is really interested, they will pay for the call. I believe a toll-free number often draws slightly interested or just curious people.
TW: If you are not marketing on the Internet, yes. It eliminates the risk and builds credibility and trust. The most important thing in cold market advertising is building trust. Do you want to do business with a guy who left his ad card in the airport bathroom?

Where do you market? (locally, nationally, internationally)
JB: All three.
JL: We market internationally. Our product focuses on the U.S. market place, but we have international members using it to move into and expand their U.S. base of operations. As long as you have a phone and an Internet connection, you can do business internationally almost as easily as locally!
DS: We market globally.
RW: Locally primarily, but nationally occasionally.

IW: All over the world. I market in every country in the world. I have no limit except the world. I love it. Just think, 6 billion people . . . I have only that limit. Wow, I love it!!
TW: Internationally.

How should someone set up their home office to maximize its effectiveness?
JB: Computer, phone, fax, modem, and voice mail.
JL: There are dozens of tools that you can use to save time and increase your effectiveness. Many of them are computer-based tools, others such as the voice mail systems and the Internet systems we have already talked about are indispensable in doing business today. Of course, one of your best tools is your phone.
DS: The more room you have the better. You will be surprised how much space even the simplest home office requires. Try to organize your space so you are in easy reach of the items you use on a regular basis. For each person working I recommend a workstation with enough space for two or three people—trust me here.
IW: Be sure to have it away from the main living area so you won't be distracted by family and TV, etc.
TW: Make it your war room. You are in a battle for freedom. Get rid of all distractions. The phone should be the center of all activity. Put your goals on the wall. Make it a very motivating place with a single focus: your freedom.

Are there any ground rules you've established for yourself, family, etc. for operating at home successfully?
JB: When you work at home you must specify the hours that you are going to work and stick to it! If you are talking to family and friends on the phone, e-mailing jokes to your buddies, and watching TV, then you are not working. You must reserve those specified hours and be working during them, just as if you had a 9-to-5 job outside your home.
JL: We've established some very simple rules. When Daddy has the headset on or is on a conference call, everyone must stay out of the office and be quiet. My two kids know that when I'm working, I'm making money that perhaps might go toward buying them a toy at Toys-R-Us. Your basic TOY-motivation strategy!
DS: There can be a high amount of stress when running a business out of your home. Stress management is very important. One rule is to grin and bear the difficult times because they are required to make your dreams a reality.
RW: Absolutely. When the business phone rings, the kids get quiet immediately.
IW: Yes, there is a time to shut off the phone that you use for business: at dinner and family times. The business phone should not be able to go 24/7. I attempt to run my business and not let my business run me. I have to work at that, but that is the goal.
TW: I live alone. The only rule I have is that I'm not allowed to interrupt myself when I'm on the telephone.

Do you consider working at home an advantage or disadvantage to your business overall?

JB: Advantage, peace of mind.

JL: I LOVE working at home! There is a BIG-TIME ADVANTAGE to having a home office. No commuting. I can work at odd hours or take spontaneous moments in the middle of the day with my family. I wouldn't be able to do this if I were in an office. I know people who literally spend two to three hours of their day on the freeways. They arrive home in a frazzled mess too tired and stressed out to enjoy what it is they are working for. My commute takes five seconds, and I have all that extra time for myself, my family, or for my business. It's great!

DS: It definitely has its advantages! The freedom alone is worth all of the stress of working from home.

RW: It is a huge advantage because I am able to put longer hours in without missing out on my boys growing up. I just take breaks more frequently when they want to spend time with me, or I finish up my paperwork after their bedtime. If anything ever comes up, my office is right there, and it is easily handled.

IW: I love working at home. Sometimes I am still in my night clothes at 3 p.m. It is wonderful.

TW: Definitely an advantage.

What parts of your work do you farm out?
JB: Very little.

JL: We hire a company to send out our information packages and product orders. They also take care of many of the administrative tasks that chew up time but don't produce direct results.

DS: Network services and search engine marketing management.

RW: At this point, my wife and I do all the work.

IW: The bill paying and the typing.

TW: Just about everything but prospecting, presenting, and training.

What part(s) do you feel should never be farmed out?
JB: Farm out accounting; never farm out customer service or advertising until you're sure they will do the job that you want. Believe it or not, in my experience, a voice mail works much better than an answering service. Never farm out phone calls.

JL: We lead many (not all) of our own conference calls. I think it is important for us to establish ourselves as leaders. I also think it's important to keep in regular contact with our top leaders. I'd personally have a hard time giving up control over our financial transactions. It is important to understand where the money is coming from and what the expense of the business is.

DS: E-mail and communications should be handled with your own personal touch.

RW: Bidding and customer relations.

IW: The personal contact with your customers. I like to keep in touch with my customer members myself.

TW: Prospecting, presenting and training.

Do you encourage or discourage... Partnerships?
JB: Discourage.
JL: I personally encourage partnerships, relationships, and joint ventures. It works for us!
DS: Definitely encourage partnerships. We run several businesses, and we are always open to new joint ventures. There is added administration involved, but two heads are better than one!
RW: Neither.
IW: I highly discourage partnerships.
TW: Discourage them. It's like a marriage. I've only seen one partnership work long-term, and they were brothers.

Do you encourage or discourage... hiring family members?
JB: Depends who they are.
JL: If the family member can do the job required, why not? However, be willing to move the work to someone more qualified as you grow.
DS: I encourage family participation. One of the great benefits of a home business is the additional family time available, and there is even more when your family is actually working with you in your business.
RW: Encourage; it teaches responsibility. I hope to bring my boys into the business one day.
IW: Yes, I do, from time to time, hire family members. However, I have agreement in writing if I do so there won't be any misunderstanding; this is very important. There are many tax advantages to hiring your family members.
TW: Encourage it.

When legal issues arise, what's your usual response?
JB: Take care of it right away. Contact the source and see if you can resolve the issue in any way before seeking council; most times you can. If not, turn it over to a lawyer right away. That's why they are there.
JL: We haven't had any problems, (knock on wood!) so I don't have a usual response!
DS: Our attorney handles legal issues, and I don't recommend anyone try taking it into their own hands. At least consult with an attorney on any legal issues.
RW: No legal issues have ever arisen.
IW: I like to let people shine at what they do. If I have a legal problem, I use an attorney right away so I have less chance of getting into trouble.
TW: Call my Pre-Paid Legal attorney immediately! It's better to prevent a legal situation before it happens. Get Pre-Paid Legal! It's only $26/month, and you get unlimited calls to an attorney and more—www.prepaidlegal.com/go/tomwood.

Does earning a lot of money improve the quality of your life, and if so, in what ways?

JB: It sure does! Peace of mind, savings, bills paid, investments, and vacations.

JL: Well, it has given us a lot more freedom, less stress, and more choices in life. We can choose where and how we want to live and the hours we want to work. I get to spend time with my family and friends. We can travel if we want. Basically, when you have money, you increase your options in life!

DS: It definitely does. Money can bring you the freedom to do the things you want to do in life without thinking twice about it. My children will not have to struggle as hard as we did growing up, and we now have the ability to literally turn dreams into reality.

RW: Money doesn't make you happy, it just eliminates most of your problems, therefore making your life much less stressful and enjoyable.

IW: Yes, yes, yes. A lot of people say money doesn't make you happy. If you notice, the people who say that are usually broke and unhappy. Also, if money doesn't make you happy, you're shopping at the wrong stores. Yes, you get happiness from a happening, and money can buy a lot of nice happenings. How about a limo for the evening? A ride on the Concord jet? A boat for the lake? Jet skis? A vacation to Spain or Italy or Australia? How about a beach house? A house at the lake? A motor home? A motorcycle? Private school for the kids? Braces for your kids teeth? A nice house for the family? Bigger diamonds for the wife or special friend? Think about it, money is what makes it all go around. I don't want anyone to think money is the most important thing; however, I believe it ranks second to oxygen. I must be clear here—happiness comes from a happening. Money can buy a lot of happenings and things. Money can't buy joy. I believe that joy and peace come from the spiritual side of our life, but money takes care of the natural things we want and desire.

TW: YES! Money does NOT make you happy. That is for sure. After my mother died last year, I took three months off and did nothing but play golf, travel, go to movies and theater, go boating, hang out on the beach, read, and write. I had the income and freedom to do what I wanted, but I was NOT happy. I believe happiness and quality of life comes from serving and leading others. Knowing that you have the freedom and resources to make a difference in peoples' lives—that's the benefit of passive income. You may find yourself financially retired in a few years, but don't ever retire from servant leadership.

Best general tax advice?

JL: Keep EXCELLENT records and hire a good CPA who understands your business. My CPA happens to also be involved in network marketing and knows all about the types of records to keep.

DS: Deductions! Deduct everything you possibly can or give your money to the government. The choice is yours. You should create a tax plan with your accountant and keep accurate records of all transactions.

RW: I use TurboTax.

IW: Keep every receipt. Get a very good bookkeeper because having a home-based business is a huge tax benefit—very big!!!

TW: Set up a corporation.

Best general investment advice?

JB: Technology mutual funds.

JL: Have a plan and stick to it! Never dip into your financial freedom account.

DS: Invest in your own business every chance you get. I would also suggest you diversify as much as possible to lessen your risk.

RW: Set aside money for your retirement as early in life as you possible can, and never tap into it. Think of your nest egg as sacred.

IW: Get out of debt totally—house and everything. For long term, I think the safest investment is mutual funds or the Dow. If you consistently put away, it won't take that long until your money will earn what you need to live on and more. I recommend everyone have at least one rental property. You just can't lose long term on real estate. They are not making any more land.

TW: Learn about money. Don't just let someone invest for you.

You're in business already, and you've just received a windfall of $20,000. What would you do with it?

JB: Increase your yearly advertising budget to use 20% of this money ($4000). Invest 20% ($4000) toward new equipment or software that your business needs. Invest $2000 into a mutual fund that's in the business' name. Put the remaining $10,000 into a money market account that's in the business name, and hold on to it for slow times of the year.

JL: I would spend the windfall on marketing. Marketing is the only way to generate new sales. That $20,000 could generate 10 times the amount in revenues or profits. Of course, you have to run the right ads, you have to test relentlessly and know what results you are getting!

DS: I would plan a getaway for my wife and children for a few days, and I would invest the rest right into our business to increase profits.

RW: Pay any outstanding debts (debt is bondage). If there is no debt, pay the normal bills and invest the rest for retirement.

IW: Pay off any charge cards, and then put the rest into a long-term mutual fund, or pick up a piece of real estate for a rental.

TW: Invest it in building systems that make it easy for others to succeed.

What do you lead with your company's products or the business opportunity?

JL: Our company's main product is pre-qualified leads. Basically, anyone in a network-marketing company needs leads, so it is very natural and easy to lead with the products.

DS: Products come first; if your prospect is not interested in your products, then I can't see how they can promote them 100%.

IW: Product always. The strength of a company is the price and the value of the product. Otherwise, it is a money game, and that is usually short term.

TW: Either. But it's usually the opportunity.

Rank the following traits in order of their importance in building a successful network marketing business: enthusiasm, persistence, knowledge, communication skills.

JL: Enthusiasm, communication skills, persistence, and knowledge.

DS: Persistence, knowledge, communication skills, and enthusiasm.

IW: Knowledge, enthusiasm, communication, and persistence. Having knowledge about the product causes enthusiasm, which enables you to effectively communicate, and if you're persistent, you will succeed.

TW: Enthusiasm, persistence, communication skills, and knowledge.

RW: Has anyone ever ranked enthusiasm anything but first?

How long were you in network marketing before you saw your first four-figure commission check? Five-figure check?
JL: It took us three months to achieve our first four-figure check and five years to get our first five-figure check.
DS: Three months. Five-figure check—one year.
IW: I received the first four-figure weekly check in the first 60 days. The five-figure check took a bit longer. I was working for five months before I saw my first five-figure weekly check.
TW: Six months. Five-figure check—two years

What's more important: the initial contact with a prospect or the follow-up?
JL: Initial contact is critical, but sales are usually made in the follow-up. Of the two, I'd say follow-up.
DS: Both are equally important. Your first impression should be memorable, but you should also follow-up at least eight to 12 times!
IW: The initial contact and the way you do it. However, if you don't follow up, you will strike out anyway. So both go hand-in-hand to complete the cycle.
TW: Which came first, the chicken or the egg?

You've just recruited a promising new distributor: how do you help them get off to a good start? Or do you consider that the new distributor's responsibility?
JL: We plug them into the system. It's their responsibility to listen to the first few conference training calls and read the manuals provided. Then we get together (in person or over the phone) and go over questions and strategy. It usually boils down to the fact that the ones who ask the questions and who show up to the meetings are the ones who will succeed.
DS: Make sure they are trained properly. The training you do in the beginning with your distributor will play a crucial role in their success. Make sure they understand everything there is to know about your business opportunity, including the marketing.
IW: The very first thing I do (within one minute) is help the new person find someone to get involved on their team. I don't feel I have been successful until the new person is earning money. That is the job of this industry—to duplicate, not just get people in and leave them to figure it out. I believe that is one of the reasons for my success. I am determined to help as many people succeed as possible.
TW: I make them independent as soon as possible. It's the only way they will ever succeed. I teach them about the systems. I encourage them when they are down. I inspire them to do more when they succeed. But I never do it for them.

How do you get your best leads?
JL: Our company is ProSTEP, and they specialize in lead generation for network marketing. We simply use our own products! What could be better?
DS: Advertising through as many avenues as possible and follow-up. As soon as a lead comes, we start our follow-up process. If they are serious about a business opportunity, they will have several opportunities to evaluate it before making their decision.
IW: I go to my warm market, and then to the people's warm market, and then to those people's warm market. I also talk to everyone I meet whom I feel would benefit from the product and/or the opportunity.
TW: 1. Referrals. There is trust built in. 2. Internet. It's just so easy.

I'm planning a big local meeting. What's the best way to fill the room?

JL: This is what I'd do. Buy 1,000 local leads from ProSTEP and have the service phone each one leaving an exciting message on their voice-mail. Then send an e-mail using our special software to all 1,000 people as a follow up. Then, because they are local to you, start calling as many as you can. Just dial away and get a commitment from them to show up!

RW: Make it fun—use contests, dinners, guest speakers, etc. In fact, anything you can do to liven up a dull meeting will draw a larger crowd.

IW: Talk about it to all my team members and encourage all to bring just one. Some will bring more, but if you have 100 local people, and they all bring one, you will have a good turn out.

TW: 100 people get five each instead of one will get 500 people.

I need to generate a hundred leads within 60 days. What's my best strategy to achieve this?

JL: Become a Premier member with ProSTEP. This will get you 2,100 leads within 60 days. If you implement an e-mail, post card, or phone campaign, you could recruit more people than you would know what to do with. This is exactly what we do and what we teach!

DS: I would start by buying leads, starting a mailing campaign online, buying targeted traffic, etc. If you are marketing offline, try to talk to as many people as you can for the next 60 days; leads will naturally occur as you meet more people.

IW: If I needed to find 100 people to talk to about my business in 60 days, I would begin by listing family, friends, relatives, acquaintances, and strangers—like people at church, people at the health club, your children's teachers at school, your barber or hairdresser . . . anyone you come into contact with every day. If they are breathing, they qualify as a potential lead.

TW: Get 10 of your friends to give you 10 of their friends' names. If you are out of friends, it's going to cost you money, and you are going to have to build trust quickly. Take out a local newspaper ad, Internet ad, national newspaper ad. But when you get a lead, get them to give you their top 20 friends' names.

How many distributors must a person recruit each month to succeed in network marketing?

JL: I would say if you can recruit eight to 10 new members per month you'll do just great. However, with our systems and leads, MANY of our clients are recruiting eight to 10 new reps per week or MORE!

DS: One never knows. You might pick up two people a month for six months, and then one will turn into a recruiting machine. I don't think it's a matter of how many recruits you sign up but their quality.

IW: I don't think it is a certain number. The important thing is to help the ones you sponsor to make money, and if you do, then you don't have to sponsor a lot of people. If you sponsor two the first month, and they sponsor two the second month, now you have four. If those four sponsor two, you have eight. If those eight sponsor two, you have 16. If this continues for just 12 months, you would have over 8,000 people in your group. However, the success name of this game is to teach people to do what you do, not see how many people you can sponsor.

TW: 10 to 30 in the first 90 days, then two to five per month after that.

Best tips for surviving rejection?

JL: Use the system to do the initial sifting and sorting. ONLY work with people who call you and chase you down to get started. I hate rejection, just like the next guy, but I haven't made a cold call for five years. Instead, the only people I talk to are those that have seen my info or visited my Website, are ready to get started, but only have a couple of questions. Rejection is no longer even in the picture!

DS: Don't take it personally. They are not rejecting you, just your opportunity.

IW: Don't take the "No" personally. Just keep going. They are not rejecting you, they are rejecting what you have to offer. So what? Some will, some won't, so what!! Next! It is a numbers game, period.

TW: Think of yourself as a waiter/waitress serving coffee. She doesn't cry when someone says they don't want coffee. He doesn't come home exhausted and think, "I don't think I can go another day without someone wanting coffee." They just keep asking, "Do you want coffee?" So just keep asking, "Do you keep your business options open?" and "Do you see an opportunity here?" If they say no, they're not rejecting you; they just don't want coffee right now.

Do you recommend that new distributors prospect close friends and family?

JL: Sure, it's fine to get your friends and family on your products, but quite honestly, the friends and family route is slow and agonizing. Besides, if they wanted to make extra money, they'll let you know. I personally would rather go after the "cold market."

DS: If your friends and family truly enjoy the product or service and are sincerely interested in the company and not just helping out a family member, then yes, I recommend family and friends.

IW: I tell you what, if my family found something that would make them big money, and they did not tell me, I would be very upset. If you love someone, you will bring good into their lives—lots of it. I tell everyone. If I am ashamed of what I do, then I should do something else. I will tell the most influential people I know, as well as the ones I love.

TW: Absolutely! At the very least you need to show them what you are doing. But don't rely on their involvement for your success. Your success will be because of you, not because of your family, friends or even your upline or downline. When you get that, you get the business.

In five years I'll be....
JB: A millionaire.
JL: I'll be a multi-millionaire.
DS: Working part time, building a private retreat, and spending quality time with my family.
RW: Debt free.
IW: In five years, I will be many times a millionaire, but more important, I will have helped many to be millionaires.
TW: Having massive positive impact on the world and my community.

In ten years I'll be...
JB: Retired.
JL: Retired as a multi-millionaire.
DS: Retired and exploring life!
RW: Financially independent.
IW: Traveling the world. I do some of that now, but I will do it full time then or as much as I want. I will spend all my summers on the lake. I love boating and the warm water, especially Lake Shasta in California.
TW: The first U.S. Senator to have a thriving network-marketing business.

What most motivates you in building your business?
JB: Watching it go up and improve and seeing how it's helping others achieve what they want.
JL: Well, it USED to be money. But now that the survival issues have been well taken care of, what really gets me going is seeing a new member suddenly "get it" and simply take off. It is so cool to be able to coach them, help them channel their enthusiasm, and then see their success! It's great to be a success coach!
DS: Knowing that in a few short years, our family will be financially independent, and we can retire to really enjoy what life has to offer.
RW: Security.
IW: The love of meeting people, being with people, and helping them to succeed.
TW: Seeing the impact the business has on people, discovering more about myself, and learning and growing.

How often do you read books and/or listen to or watch tapes for improving your business skills or knowledge?
JL: In the first two years in this business, I literally listened to tapes for two hours a day. Dan Kennedy, various network marketing trainers, Jim Rohn, Anthony Robbins, Earl Nightingale. Steven Covey, and Jay Abraham. Right now, I spend time every day reading business magazines and business-development information on the Internet.
DS: I read as much as I can. I try to learn as much as I can without suffering information overload.
IW: I read books and listen to tapes daily. I also, as things become available, go to and hear motivational speakers from around the world.
TW: I read great books daily. My car always has an audio cassette/CD program on personal development in it. I attend a one-day seminar each month. I attend a one-weekend seminar each quarter. I attend a one-week seminar each year. If I can't attend a seminar, I teach one.

The most underrated activity in business is?
JB: Tracking your advertising.

JL: Getting on the phone and using it elegantly. You can make personal calls, conference calls, and three-way calls, use your voice mail box, use the fax functions, utilize 800 numbers, and use calling services.

DS: I would not say activity but people. The ordinary person in business often gets very little recognition, yet many top businesses would crumble without them.

IW: I believe that three-way calling is the most overlooked method in which to build an network-marketing business. It seems like the third party brings magic to the ability to interest the new prospect.

TW: Personal recruiting. It solves every problem you have in your network-marketing business.

The most overrated activity in business is?

JL: Face-to-face prospecting meetings or presentations.

DS: Marketing online. Too many people think starting a home business on the Internet is a quick route to easy street. It takes hard work and determination to succeed at a home business. Much more work than most people realize.

IW: I believe mass direct mailings, post cards, and the like are rated far higher than the results they bring.

TW: Organizing to get ready. Just do it!

If I had to start my business all over again, what would you do differently?

JB: Have an attorney look at my terms of service.

JL: Honestly, I could not say what I would do anything differently. Anytime there was a bump in the road, we treated it like a learning experience and got mileage out of it that way.

DS: Not a thing! The steps I have taken and failures experienced along the way needed to occur for us to become successful.

IW: Because of the nature of the business, I would work harder sooner. To begin with, you are underpaid (most people become discouraged with this). But if you work very hard, you are soon overpaid. It took me nine months to get to $65,000 a month. If I had worked harder from the beginning, I could have been there sooner. And one thing I have found is that sooner is better than later, and more is better than less (referring to money), and easier is better than harder. Many people spend all their time starting and stopping, so they take too long to get momentum going, and in this game, the goal is to get to momentum as soon as possible.

TW: When I got started a very successful man in network marketing told me not to spend time with the people who didn't really want success. I wish I had listened to him.

What was your worst business decision?

JB: To have a partner.

JL: Front loading myself with thousands of dollars of product in my first network-marketing business just to make "manager." It wasn't a good business decision, but it was a learning experience in what not to do.

DS: Doing taxes and accounting tasks by ourselves. Trust me—seek out a professional accountant, even if it's just for consulting. The time it saves you will be well worth the fees.

RW: Buying a new overpriced laptop before the company could afford it.

IW: To hesitate to get into this industry sooner. It is the fastest way to wealth that I know.

TW: I spent a lot of money trying to recruit a famous TV personality. I got him in the business, but he expected me to do all the work. I'd rather have a janitor with desire than a CEO with ego.

What was your best business decision?
JB: To get rid of my partner. To turn my service into an opportunity that others can join and sell my products and services with me.

JL: Teaming up with my partner, Andy Hummel, and starting our WBI business. We have different personalities, and we have set things up so that each of us are using our strengths to build the business.

DS: Starting our corporation and choosing to run it from home.

RW: Returning the same laptop and getting an LS-120 drive for back up.

IW: To get started in the current business I am in. The Internet is where it's at.

TW: To be in business for myself full-time.

What do you consider to be the main keys of your success?
JB: Hard work, determination, and the drive to make it the ultimate success. Never give up. If at first you don't succeed, try, try again!

JL: Being willing to think out of the box. Instead of following the crowd and following the mainstream, be a rebel in the way you think about business. Whatever Madison Avenue is doing, do the opposite. I try to think out of the box every time I move into a different area or expand the business.

DS: Learning from the mistakes I have made in the past. Having a supportive spouse is also a big key to my success.

RW: The economy has exploded with new construction. I was in the right place at the right time.

IW: The key is to help other people to be successful. As Zig Ziglar has said, "If you help enough people get what they want, you will get what you want."

TW: I was climbing Mount Fuji and passed an old lady in her 90s who had been climbing for five days. I asked her the secret of her success. She told me to get out of the way; she was climbing the mountain. Either she was very cranky or she meant for me to learn that all distractions are equal. Keep climbing.

What's your success philosophy?
JB: It can only become what I make of it! I do not wait for my ship to come in. I swim out and meet it!

JL: I know this is cliché, but it is true: Help enough people achieve their dreams and you will get what you want. This is what it boils down to in this business.

DS: Don't stop until you have made your goals! If you are persistent, you will succeed. Failure is quitting. Don't be a quitter!

RW: I do WHATEVER IT TAKES to get the job done and get it done right.

IW: As I help people become successful and achieve their goals, my success will be guaranteed. I also believe that you must make a business plan and follow the plan with absolute consistency and persistence to achieve your desired results.

TW: There is no other way to build massive long-term wealth than to deserve it. The income you receive from your business is directly proportional to the value you put in peoples' lives. To build wealth and add value, you must become a leader. There are many leadershipstyles and strategies for you to choose from. It's your company and your decision on how you want to lead, but you must lead. I believe a great leader must be a servant leader. One who leads by example and serves the people.

What about you has changed the most since finding success in business?
JB: Attitude! I used to feel sorry for myself, thinking that everything I tried to do just wouldn't work for "me," like I was the only one. Why was it working for so many others and not me? Little did I know that it was all a learning experience. Just like first through 12th grade. Teachers would not give 12th-grade math problems to first graders. You must work up to that gradually. Failure is not bad when you learn from it. The word "failure" is really just a disguise for the lesson learned. If you can learn from failure you will be a success, because you first must learn what not to do in order to learn what is needed to be done.
JL: Confidence.
DS: I find that we are more giving now; there is a certain amount of gratification in being able to help others less fortunate. If more people helped their fellow man, this crazy world we live in would be a much better place.
RW: Financial security has given me some additional peace of mind.
IW: I have become more patient because helping people can be a challenge, but as I stick in there with them, I have become a better and more patient person.
TW: One day, after years of struggle and tears and failure in the business, my father looked at me and said, "Tom, I believe in you." I began to cry. I needed to hear that so bad, because I didn't believe in myself at the time. I've learned that you can only tell others that you believe in them if you believe in yourself first.

What is the legacy you hope to leave?
JB: To be known as a person who's goal it was to do the best he could to better others.
JL: I don't have this big dream of saving the world or anything like that. I just want to make sure my wife and kids and my other loved ones are taken care of for life. It's amazing what having money can do!
DS: Hopefully I can create a path for others to follow along. If I can help one person succeed in business and help them create a new easier way of life, as I have done for our family, then it was all worth it!
RW: The legacy I hope to leave to my kids has nothing to do with work. I hope my kids think of me as a God-fearing Christian man who founded their faith by presenting my life as a living sacrifice to Jesus Christ. In common words, I want my kids to know that the only way to truly have joy in their lives is for them to have a relationship with Jesus Christ. Having money doesn't fulfill your life, BUT adding money to an already fulfilled life is indescribable.
IW: I would like to be remembered as a person who wasn't interested in just his own goals, but desired to help other people achieve their goals and dreams by being available to help them.
TW: In my mother's honor and my father's name, I intend to look as many people in the eye as possible and tell them that I believe in them.

To **Contact** Our Interviewees...

Colleen Abbott
American Fork, UT
888-722-2688
801-492-0787
colleen@noni.com

Joe Brennan
Cary, NC
919-854-5544
919-233-9933
joeb@iypdirect.com
http://www.iypdirect.com

Glen Brink
Boulder, CO
303-442-6460
303-413-0450
glenbrink@unforgettable.com

Larry Edwards
Everett, WA
425-317-8229
425-317-8329
ceodad@firetrail.com

Carol Ely
Corbin, KY
606-528-1582
606-528-8731
elroy@tcnet.net

Ray Gebauer
Bellevue, WA
888-882-8949
425-603-9648
rgebauer@premier1.net
http://www.cureanydisease.com

To **Contact** Our Interviewees...

Johnny Keller
Wernerville, NC
828-658-8141
828-658-8743

Joseph Lemire
Akron, OH
727-586-0424
727-588-0443
mike@pplassociate.com

Jean Lewis
Rotonda, FL
941-698-0444
visionary@ewol.com

Jim Lewis
Monarch Beach, CA
888-MLM-PROS

John Lloyd
Scottsdale, AZ
602-494-4882
602-953-5772

Lance Lomako
Bellevue, WA
425-646-4368
425-462-1634
lance@maxxconnect.net

Jim Lutes
Encinitas, CA
760-635-0969
760-635-0968

Michael Rideout
San Diego, CA
800-455-0096
858-453-8394
michael.rideout2@gte.net

Anne Rooney
Puyallup, WA
253-845-1873
253-845-2753
arooney@unidial.com

David Seitz
Larksville, PA
570-283-9368
associatesearch@associatesearch.com

Eileen Silva
Southlake, TX
817-424-5204
817-251-1358
ensilva@aol.com

Rich Strayer
Wheat Ridge, CO
303-233-4152
303-202-9134
RichStrayer@olmktg.com

To **Contact** Our Interviewees...

Ron Wade
Certified Balance, Inc
Monroe, LA
318-325-5754
318-322-4251
1rhino@msn.com

Doug West
Moyers, OK
580-298-2778
580-298-6593
webmaster@kosoma.com

Shawn Wheeland
Aiken, SC
803-648-6880
803-641-2010
1image@bellsouth.com

Irvin Widmer
NE Salem, OR
503-463-0122
lwidmer@home.com

Ed Wiens
Caldwell, ID
208-455-2700
208-455-2900
edwiens@cyberhighway.net

Tom Wood
Ft. Lauderdale, FL
954-565-5585
tomwood@tomwood.net

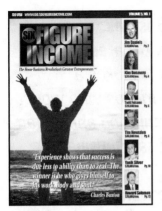

SECRETS
for building the
$100,000
home-based business

Want giant, bank account-bursting income? Then you better be emulating giant, bank account-bursting income earners! And NOBODY gives you the scoop on more six-figure-earning home business entrepreneurs than Six-Figure Income Magazine.

● We show you who's making the big bucks in home business. More importantly, SFI shows you <u>HOW</u> they're making it – the attitude, the philosophies, the actual techniques used by some of the most savvy, intelligent, and dynamic entrepreneurs on the planet. You get exact strategies, secrets, tips, and worldly-wise advice you can start using <u>right</u> <u>now</u> to build your own personal fortune at home.

● You'll learn from the masters what real freedom is all about - the money to live your dreams...and the time to actually live them!

● <u>For less than $3 a month</u>, you'll enjoy full, <u>insider access</u> to the kind of information that these movers and shakers normally charge <u>thousands of dollars</u> for.

● SFI gives you a direct pipeline to the minds of the home business super-rich and <u>it's available NOWHERE ELSE</u>! Every article in SFI is an <u>exclusive</u> –every issue a recipe for turning your small business into a BIG paycheck.

Missing a single issue could be hazardous to your wealth!

*Call **402-434-8480** to order your subscription today or order on the Web at: **www.sixfigureincome.com***

The Home Business Revolution's Greatest Entrepreneurs, Volume 2

THE EXCLUSIVE INTERVIEWS FROM SIX-FIGURE INCOME MAGAZINE

THE HOME BUSINESS REVOLUTION'S

GREATEST ENTREPRENEURS
VOLUME 2

Colleen Abbott
Joe Brennan
Glen Brink
Larry Edwards
Carol Ely
Ray Gebauer
Johnny Keller
Joseph Lemire
Jean Lewis
Jim Lewis
John Lloyd
Lance Lomako
Jim Lutes
Michael Rideout
Anne Rooney
David Seitz
Eileen Silva
Rich Strayer
Ron Wade
Doug West
Shawn Wheeland
Irvin Widmer
Ed Wiens
Tom Wood

With Forward By **GERY CARSON**

The Home Business Revolution's Greatest Entrepreneurs makes a great gift for friends who work at home or are thinking about starting a home-based business.

Are you a network marketer? Get a copy for all your downline associates.

Quantity: **Price:**

1 copy . . . . $17.95 each

2-5 copies. . . . . $15.95 each

6-24 copies. . . . . $12.95 each

25 - 49 copies. . . . . $9.95 each

Call for larger quantities

Add Shipping & Handling to above prices:

– US and Canada residents add $2 for first book; $.50 for each additional book.

– Residents of other countries add 30% of total book cost.

Order by calling *402-434-8480*
or order on the Web at: *www.sixfigureincome.com*

Mail orders can be sent to:

Carson Services, Inc., PO Box 4785, Lincoln, NE 68504 USA.

Cash, check, money order, or charge accepted. Make checks to: Carson Services, Inc.

ALL PRICES SUBJECT TO CHANGE WITHOUT NOTICE